the
ULTIMATE
guide to the
perfect
Card

prose • sentiments • poems • expressions

the
ULTIMATE
guide to the *perfect*
Card

prose • sentiments • poems • expressions

by
Linda LaTourelle

BLUE GRASS
publishing
Mayfield, Kentucky

For information write:
Blue Grass Publishing
PO Box 634
Mayfield, KY 42066 USA
service@theultimateword.com
www.theultimateword.com

ISBN: 0-9745339-5-5

1st ed.
Mayfield, KY : Blue Grass Pub., 2004

Blue Grass Publishers has made every effort to give proper ownership credit for all poems and quotes used within this book. In the event of a question arising from the use of a poem or quote, we regret any error made and will be pleased to make the necessary correction in future editions of this book. All scripture was taken from the King James Version of the Bible.

Cover Design: Todd Jones, Tennessee
CK Fraternity font used with permission by Creating Keepsakes
Proudly printed in the United States of America

10 9 8 7 6 5 4 3 2 1

Recognition

recognition\ rec`og*ni"tion\, n. the process
of recognizing something or someone by
Remembering: *"She received recognition for
her many achievements."*

To recognize the kindness and help
from others is a willful act of appreciation.

> dedicate\ded"i*cate\, v. 1. To set apart and con-
> secrate, as to a divinity, or for sacred uses; to de-
> vote formally: *"They dedicate their lifes to God."*

Dear Lord, It is with adoration and praise that I dedicate this book to you. You have poured out your blessings on it already and it is exciting to be a part of this journey. I know that you have a great purpose here and it is my prayer that if nothing else, one life may be touched by its contents.

This birth of this book is truly awesome. You have put it together with such amazing connections from around this country. Through it you have opened so many doors and blessed in ways inconceivable. Thus, it is with the greatest love that I say Thank You. My fervent prayer is for all that is accomplished as a result of this book to bring awesome Glory to you and a humbleness of spirit to myself and all who read it. I stand in awe of you.   -Linda

For my daughters—

You are the light of my life and my greatest blessing in this world. You are so incredibly talented, beautiful and precious. God gave me my heart's desire with your love. May my life be a joyful blessing and encouragement to you everyday of your life. I love you forever and always. May you continue to let your light shine for the Lord. Thank you for all of your help and patience through all of this. I know there will be many blessings for the honor you show me everyday. I love you with all my heart.

                    -Momma

Vessels of silver, and vessels of gold, . . .
which also king David did dedicate unto
the Lord. -2 Sam. viii. 10, 11

kindness\kind"ness\, n. A kind act; an act of good
will; as, to do a great kindness; an instance of kind be-
havior: *I will always remember your many kindnesses*

Todd Jones. Well, what can I say, he did it again. Words are a
mere whisper of the gratitude I feel for this man. Only a man after
God's own heart can be the blessing that he is. Todd, my writing
cannot express what my heart feels for your awesome talent and
friendship. Thank you once again for creating a masterpiece! You're
the best...as an artist, a friend and a witness for God!

The Ladies. In case you ever wondered, there truly do exist fairy god-
mothers right here on earth. I know, because I have my very own personal group of them—Garnell, Mardell, Reba, Anna Faye, Hilda, Doro-
thy, Miss Mary, Mary and Gisella. The encouragement and love I receive from them has been a gift from above for many years now. When I
have needed the warmth of a hug, the strength of a prayer, the wisdom of
experience or a gentle hand to lift me up, their faithful friendship has
always been a guiding light. It is my desire to share with the world that
the wonder of God's love exists in the simple joys of friendship. To you
my dear ladies, words do not exist that speak what my heart wants to
say. You are a treasure close to my soul. Thank you for love beyond
compare. I love you all so dearly.

Sisters. It has been quite a journey for us to reach this place, but oh, the
inexpressible joy watching how God has led us here. I am overwhelmed
with love to be sharing a passion of mine with you. I know there is a purpose in this venture far greater than any of us can see. I wanted to take
this special moment to say my love for you is overflowing. As we begin
this new road may we count the awesome blessings of being sisters not
only by birth, but by rebirth. I remember Dad always said, K.I.S.S. (keep
it simple...), so on that note...Thank You! May you be as blessed as I
am! I love you all so much!

Barbara Cox. What a joy it is to share your work with the world. Your
prayers are at last a reality. May it add a wonderful joy to your life and be
an inspiration to keep using the gift God has given you. I thank you for
your kindness and generosity in allowing me the honor of presenting your
writing to others. Your words have touched me and I know they will others. May you be abundantly blessed through all of this. Thank you.

"True kindness is a gift that cannot be given with
anything of this world." -Linda LaTourelle

thanks\thanks\ pl.n. Grateful feelings or thoughts; gratitude: a heart full of thanks. An expression of gratitude; a note of thanks to a contributor: *"He gave thanks to God."*

Thanks is such a small word when one desires to express tremendous gratitude to special people for their kindness. It is nothing short of a miracle that this book has come together so quickly. But when you have the ULTIMATE Guide that I do, how could I expect anything else. I am blessed by a multitude of friends.

From the writings within, the proof reading, the typing, the contributions, the prayers and more, God has put together a special collection of thoughts and feelings to enable it's readers to be inspired and take from the pages words that might bless others.

In no particular order, my heartfelt thanks to:

Dan LaTourelle	*Todd Jones*
Thena Smith	*My girls*
Barbara Cox	*My Sisters*
C.C. Milam	*My parents*
August Jones	*Dee Gruenig*
Sherry Moss	*Warren Gruenig*
The Ladies	*Jeff Vann*
Anna Faye	*Nicole McKinney*
Lynne Rogers	*My brothers*
Holly VanDyne	*Simply Sentiments*
Brandy Tucker	*Shirley Tessier*

No act of kindness, no matter how small, is ever wasted. -Aesop

Table of Contents

Table of Contents

NOTES HERE

Sentiments

These are the feelings deep in
my heart, filling my soul
with words to impart.
How do I tell you in so many
ways, I'm sorry, Congrats, or
Hip Hip hooray? Love that is
heartfelt & romance so rare—
Oh, how many feelings I
am longing to share.
So what's in a word
and where do I start?
With wisdom and love that
comes straight from my heart!

-Linda LaTourelle © 2004
and Thena, my dear friend
Thanks for the finishing touch!

Going to take
a sentimental journey~

Cardmaking: Using a flat piece of stiff paper or cardboard, adding embellishments to create a greeting card which has verses to express particular sentiments or feelings

If you can talk you really can write. but now that you have this book it will most certainly simplify things for you. The words within this book are meant to inspire, uplift and cheer all who peruse it's pages. You can use it to create just about any type of card you find necessary. May it touch your life and the lives of others in a very special way.   -Linda

■ ■

Words, thoughts and heartfelt sentiments—these are the memories that linger long after the event or occasion. Your love for someone special portrayed in the ink upon the paper by your touch. Oh, what a joy to behold.

Have you ever gone to your mailbox and discovered a handwritten envelope from someone special? It's such a cherished gift, a lasting treasure! What is even better is to open that envelope and discover that someone you know took the time to pen warm, loving sentiments to you. While many people will just write their thoughts within a ready-made card from a store, others will use a blank note card and yet others will give a handmade creation. Whatever the choice, their ultimate desire is to share their heart.

Creating cards is becoming a fast growing hobby, with designer books and magazines specific to the market now available. With scrapbooking so big in the industry, the cardmaking was certain to have a natural following. Add to that, the growth of the rubberstamp companies, and the potential is awe inspiring, limited only by the imagination of the cardmaker.

With the Internet so accessible, e-cards have become one of the preferred methods of communication with family and friends. While convenient to send off a quick e-card or postcard, nothing can replace the loving feeling upon receiving a handmade card. Unfortunately we neglect to do the most simple and meaningful things because of the fast paced life most people live. However, there is nothing that can speak to the heart of your loved ones the way something you have created personally for them can.

In gathering items for my scrapbook albums, one of the most cherished mementos for me to come across is a note or card from someone I love. The ones I hold particularly close are the cards and notes from my children and those from family members no longer with us. When I stop to read a card made in grade school by one of my daughters it brings to me a soul-soothing smile as I reflect upon the fond memories of those earlier days. I find a familiar handwritten letter from my great-grandmother and I think about her loveliness and sweetness. I remember how I miss her and how long ago she went home to be with the Lord. The joy I feel as I read through these precious treasures again and again brings tears of joy and love. What a flood of memories fill my soul as I look at the feelings expressed by my loved ones in these simple sentiments.

I know from personal experience, there are many times in life that finding just the right card is so important. I remember times that an occasion would arise and I could spend an hour or more in the card section of a store or perhaps several stores looking for what I had in mind. There were times it was hard to find that perfect card, too, and even times when I just couldn't. So then it would mean going home and trying to come up with something on my own either on the computer or by creating a handmade card. My children have always made their own cards–they receive a blessing in creating them. It allows them to express their love in an artistic way and that is a joy for them.

■ ■

There are so many wonderful papers, inks and products now on the market, you can embellish your heart out. Making cards is pure delight! Years ago I was involved quite a bit with rubberstamping, but due to many other things there was little time left to really explore the possibilities. I recently went to a craft show and was so impressed with the amazing card creations by some local rubberstampers. Such beauty was in these delicate works of art and then to add to them heart-felt expressions, these cards become irreplaceable pieces that will keep on giving to the recipients for generations to come. Rubberstamping has come a long way in the last twenty years.

With the blending of scrapbooking and rubberstamping, cardmaking is limited only by your imagination. There are many good articles in magazines about cardmaking and even a few books out there about techniques, lots of products, too. Good news, for cardmakers–there is a great new magazine designed specifically for the cardmaker, "Simply Sentiments". More information in the "Resource" section of this book.

Would you like to open your mailbox and find love in a simple envelope? Well, let it start with you and trickle on out. Within this book are words that have come down through the generations. Words that still inspire even now. There are also words from today created with the same passion as those of long ago. And, if you search these pages, you will see more in these perfect words. You will see your words, hidden within this book, hidden within your heart. Words ready to leap off the page or out of your heart to honor another in some particular way.

18

■■■■■■■■■■■■■■■■■■■■■■■■■■■

Trust

your heart! Pray about the occasion for which you need a card. Read the book, search your heart, understand in your mind what it is you want to convey. The words WILL come just believe that sentiments of our heart are often revealed in the quietness of mind and spirit. You will know when the words are right and when they are, there is no gift that can bless more in this incredible way.

So begin today, as you come across places in this book that touch you, highlight them. If you feel they are words relevant to a particular person or situation, make notations. Use this book and allow it to inspire you. I know you will come to a place where you find your words and in doing so your life will be touched.

Here are the feelings

From deep in my heart

Words from my soul

That I long to impart.

Words of love so heartfelt

That I long to share

Some read like poetry

...others a prayer....

-Thena Smith © 2004

H ere are some thoughts about cards. When you receive a card do you find it difficult to throw it away? I have a collection of the really special ones from those close to me. The ones I treasure most are those with handwritten sentiments. To me, cards that someone took the time to create and share their heart are the greatest blessings. It's very difficult to throw away something that you know was a gift of love.

I want to take a moment to share about a card that was such a surprise and an amazing blessing. About ten years ago, on our move to Kentucky, my father blew my socks off with his creation given to me on my birthday. Now you see, my dad is a great salesman, golfer, intellectual, but never have I known him as a man with artistic ability of the cardmaking kind. I don't know what inspired him the day he created a handmade masterpiece, but I will treasure it always. He used a manila file folder and covered it with pictures gathered from the beautiful Country magazines and others he found. He wrote in his own hand sentiments that touched my very soul. It was a special blessing. He never liked store bought cards and really wasn't the sentimental type, so he would always encourage my mother to create her own. When my sister, in California, became partners in a scrapbook store she got our mother interested in scrapbooking and eventually creating cards. I am so blessed, because every card she gives now is handmade with her love and artistic ability. It's been a wonderful blessing for her, also, as she creates individual cards for all of her children and grandchildren. I cherish each and every card I have received from her. Now each time I look at these cards and I see her handwriting, I know the love behind it.

When I close my eyes I can picture her in my mind's eye sitting at her table creating these little gems. Sweet blessings from my mother's heart. Thanks Mom and Dad—you are a treasure!

■■■■■■■■■■■■■■■■■■■■■■■■■■■■■■■■

Now, back to my point, which I guess I just made. Throwing away a handmade card is next to impossible. The recipient will always value the love that went into it. Think about cards your children made when they were little. Did it break your heart to toss it? Or do you tuck them away, like me? Now that you know all this, think of the blessing you are giving with the gift of a handmade card to that someone special.

Just like scrapbooking, or any craft for that matter, not everyone is really artistically inclined or wants to be. But in cardmaking, things are a bit different. Cards can be created using the simplest of tools and designs. You are only limited by your imagination.

Imagination is the soul within
-Linda LaTourelle

Imagination? You say that you don't have one? (or at least you think you don't)! No more excuses– with cardmaking you can K.I.S.S. (keep it simple...). The design on your card can be created in a matter of seconds with a few rubber stamps, your computer or you can utilize the techniques available through many sources now on the market. There are some lovely full color books out there about cardmaking techniques that will teach you step by step. A new website to visit for cardmakers is *www.simplysentiments.com*. Just go to your local scrapbook or rubberstamp store and ask for books and magazines or classes that are specific to making cards. One thing to remember is to relax and have fun, (color outside the lines) that will show in the ultimate creation of your masterpiece of love.

21

CARDMAKING TOOLS

- The Ultimate Guide to the Perfect Card–is definitely a must have for an abundance of verses and poems for the perfect sentiments

- Pens...lots of them, different colors, thicknesses, shapes, types, metallic, watercolor, charcoal, etc.

- Templates...there are an abundance available to create all shapes and sizes of cards and notes for every occasion, remember the great software, too

- Keep a pocket size thesaurus and dictionary with all your cardmaking tools. I am always referring to the thesaurus so I don't keep repeating myself. It also helps to get the creative juices flowing and expands your vocabulary at the same time.

- Paper...varying sizes, colors, textures, shapes, thicks and thins; velum and gloss, too, envelopes

- Chalks to use for that extra soft look

- Decorative scissors and punches

- Paper cutter...mini size works for most cutting

- Accordion folder...keeps papers organized

- Notebook to list favorite quotes or jot down ideas and thoughts that come to you.

- Rubberstamps, Die cuts, Eraser, White Out, etc.

- Embellishments of your choosing

- Stickers, glue, ribbon, lace, glitter, jewels, etc.

CARD MAKING TIPS

◎ Set up a special place just for you to work on your cardmaking projects. Make the ambiance soft and inviting, too. Try some soft music, a scented candle and some aromatic tea to sip as you allow your imagination to seek the perfect design and wording. Be sure to have a chair that is proper for your body and plenty of table space with good lighting to ensure comfort.

◎ Cardmaking is good for the soul, so consider this an enchanting time of being alone with yourself.

◎ Find a quiet place to sit and create. Solitude enhances creativity, allowing feelings to flow

◎ If you get stuck on what to write:
~refer to the tips in my book
~think about who you are creating for
~take a break and sip some tea
~ask yourself what your heart wants to say

◎ Think about the person for whom you are creating the card to determine the type of card you want to create. Make a list of all the cards you will be needing to send this year and add some extra

◎ Try to make several cards at once if they are for similar events. You can personalize them for each occasion, but this will give you selection on hand when the need arises. It's also just as easy to create several of the same card at one time

◎ Don't forget to decorate the envelope, too. It adds to the uniqueness of the card

23

Thena's Thoughts

For those people not fluent enough to write letters and mushy notes, a card is an acceptable means of expressing everything from love to humor. Often we know what feelings we want to express but are at a loss for words. True, there is nothing new under the sun, for down through history men and women have shared these same feelings and since the beginning of the creating and exchanging of cards, these feelings have been expressed. But we're always looking for something different.

Almost everyday I get requests for verses for birthdays, new baby congratulations, a thank you to teacher, friend or pastor. The writer usually prefaces it with "I just cannot write", but" and then pours out beautiful thoughts from their heart. They have written the verse in their hearts but just need help getting it down on paper.

As you write your card, whether prose or poetry, think about what you want to say, what does the person mean to you and what do you feel in your heart. If you write down even a few key words, you can go back and elaborate on your thoughts.

If I have a request for a special card for a wedding, an engagement, sympathy, or special birthday card, I ask God to give me something that will touch that person's heart and express what they want to say and what the recipient needs to hear. Many times I receive notes back asking me how I knew what their hopes, fears or dreams were and my answer is that I didn't, but God knows and I still think it is amazing that in this vast universe He still will answer my little requests to bless someone with a special verse.

24

Poems

Sentiments

Quotes

and

Expressions

■ ■

The History of the Greeting Card

The modern custom of sending greeting cards can be traced back through the centuries. The valentine is considered to be the original ancestor of today's greeting cards. The Germans printed New Year's greetings from woodcuts as early as the year 1400.

Esther A. Howland was a pioneer in the American valentine manufacturing industry. In 1847, she became fascinated with the idea of making valentines using scraps of paper, lace and ribbons. With the help of her friends, she was America's first assembly-line producer of high-quality lacy valentines.

Louis Prang, in Boston, is primarily credited with the start of the greeting card industry in America. In the early 1870s, he began the publication of deluxe editions of Christmas cards, which found a ready market in England. In 1875, Prang introduced the first complete line of Christmas cards to the American public.

By the late 1950s, there were hundreds of greeting card publishers who produced about five billion cards, with half of those being Christmas cards. Over seven billion greeting cards for all occasions are purchased annually in the United States.

Handmade cards have come full circle. We are taking our cue from Esther Howland and using our "scraps" to craft personal works of art for our family and friends.

A sincere thanks to "Simply Sentiments" magazine for their generosity in allowing us to share excerpts from this article in their premiere issue debuting January/February 2004. For the complete article, please be sure to visit them online www.simplysentiments.com or contact them through the information in the "Resource" section of this book.

■■■■■■■■■■■■■■■■■■■■■■■■■■■■■■■■■■

Expressing Yourself

The perfect card should communicate, celebrate and commemorate the occasion for which it was created to the person it was created for.

Communicate: \Com*mu"ni*cate\, v 1. To impart; to bestow; to convey 2. transmit thoughts or feelings

To impart your feelings should be the goal in your card. Letting the recipient know that you are with him in spirit and emotion on whatever occasion this might be is important. So many times we receive generic cards, with generic sentiments and never really know what the sender is feeling. Through this simple card you can express a range of emotions from affection, ardor, concern or desire to elation, grief, passion or sympathy. So making communication of your feelings the main focus in your cardmaking will result in a blessing to the recipient.

Celebrate: \Cel"e*brate\, v. 1. To observe an event or day with ceremonies of respect, festivity, or rejoicing.

The card you create should reflect the mood of the occasion. Is it a solemn, joyous, miraculous, passionate or spiritual time? Whatever the mood, the concept of your card should symbolize the event through color, design, embellishment and sentiment. At a glance, your heartfelt emotions will speak to the heart of the recipient and evoke feelings relative to the occasion, through your design. Everyone wants to feel special, no matter what the tone of an event. We all need to feel like we matter and nothing says that more than the giving of our time. The fact that you would take the time to create something totally unique to the event says so much about your heart.

■■■■■■■■■■■■■■■■■■■■■■■■■■■■■■■

Commemorate: Com*mem"o*rate\, v. 1. To call to remembrance by a special act or observance; to celebrate with honor and solemnity; to honor, as a person or event, by some act of respect or affection, intended to preserve the remembrance of the person or event. 2. keep alive the memory of someone

Think of how often we search for the perfect words to say or write, or the perfect gift to buy. For many of us, it is important that a particular event or time be kept close to our hearts. Think about picture taking. We all want pictures that will capture a specific moment. So it is with a card. Let your card capture the moment and be a cherished memory that can be touched and remembered for generations to come. Whatever the occasion, because that moment was a special time in the history of the recipient's life, you will want to express the importance by incorporating all of the above elements in your creations.

Card making allows you to be creative and express yourself with a very personal touch. There are a host of occasions where a handmade card would be a wonderful gesture. From Anniversaries, to Birthdays, to Weddings and more, cards can be created using the simplest of techniques and products or you can get elaborate and create an elegant piece of art. Either way, because you took the time to make it, the recipient will feel very special.

Technique is limited only by your imagination. There are some basics to remember that will add to a more attractive card. I won't elaborate much here, because there are many books, magazines and websites available that will take you to new heights in your cardmaking techniques and keep you apprised of the latest in trendy and traditional products for all your cardmaking needs and wants.

For those of you into scrapbooking and rubber-stamping, you already know the endless supplies available to create the perfect page and thus it's a natural to transfer these same techniques and use the same products for cardmaking. For those who are not familiar with these wonderful crafts, you're in for a treat. Being a newcomer to the scrapping world, there appears to be an endless supply of products that would allow you to create a magnificent masterpiece. Finding these products and learning about techniques is easy, too. It's just like being a kid in a candy store.

For starters, visiting your local scrapbook or rubber stamp stores will introduce you to such an incredible array of products and educational materials to create projects such as cards, note cards, gift tags, gift wrap, bookmarks, certificates, awards, invitations and so much more. Many stores hold classes on a regular basis to help educate, as well as share the experience with fellow crafters.

While you're at the stores, it would benefit you to check out the latest in magazines available that can teach you and treat you to the latest and greatest materials you might want. Listed in the Resource section of my book is information about a few of the popular magazines available. Be sure to check them out, especially Simply Sentiments, the brand new magazine designed specifically with cardmakers in mind.

■■■■■■■■■■■■■■■■■■■■■■■■■■■■

Once you've explored all the stores in your area and still need more materials, be sure to get online and visit all the online stores. I've listed a few in the Resource section for your convenience, but there are so many that it is impossible for me to list them all. Sometimes you can find things online that aren't available anywhere else and vice versa.

Now that you have all your materials (o. k., a few), you're probably wondering where to begin. Well, once you've read all you can in the magazines you've acquired, attended every class in nine counties of local rubberstamping and scrapbooking stores, never fear there's more yet!

When I started writing my book and researching this pastime, I was in absolutely blown away by the endless amount of information and products available through the Internet for all of you cardmaking, rubberstamping and scrapbooking addicts. If you want to learn technique, there are unlimited people on the web showcasing talents and explaining the techniques used to create their latest new creations.

There are also an abundance of newsletters and magazines are available only online. Some are available for free, others for a nominal fee. I believe most are open to accepting submissions from their readers, too, which makes it wonderful for a newcomer to this craft, because the ideas presented are almost unlimited. The talent that is abounding is awe-inspiring, too. Again, I have listed a few in my Resource section for your convenience.

Then when you still want more, you will definitely want to check out some of the message boards for tips and techniques from the amateurs and the professionals. Many of the major magazines and some of the big companies have their own boards, as do the smaller online stores. There are also message boards that are just that and nothing more.

To be honest, there are so many resources available for cardmakers, scrappers and stampers to create a card by hand or on their computer, I am learning about them all the time. It's a good thing they weren't all stores in my neighborhood, because I would get lost. Lost, but I'd be having fun shopping, too! The point is that you'll have fun with all the window-shopping you can do.

My first suggestion–create a list of specific cards you want to make throughout the year and begin to create a detailed list of necessary supplies and a wish list, too. Keep them in a small notebook and carry it with you on your shopping sprees, whether it's traveling to a local store or elsewhere or simply your online surfing ventures. You will find that this will save you time and money and help you to avoid purchasing duplicate materials. In a sense it's kind of like buying clothes. While it's all well and good to have a variety of clothes in an array of colors, styles, shapes and sizes, if you don't have some coordination and semblance of organization, it can become a very confusing time selecting an outfit, to say nothing of the potential for being on the worst-dressed list for the year. Seriously, how many times have you gone to your closet with an article of clothing in hand and guess what, there's nothing

31

that matches. I have literally given away items after years with the tags still on because of this very thing. I must say that my scrapbook armoire, in my living room, was beginning to look that way until I decided to try to plan ahead. I can tell you this makes for a more peaceful time when I finally to get down to creating my projects and saves me money, also.

I hope this tip helps, so when you go shopping you will have a plan. I'm not saying don't buy those sweet little doodads that you love and know will look so beautiful on "something", I'm just suggesting if one has a plan, they will be economically better off than if you just shop so impulsively.

Now let's see what are the basics to have to make this fun and inspiring time–

- ◎ Your little space with a comfortable table or desk and chair
- ◎ Warm and inviting with good lighting all around
- ◎ Soft music to help the creative juices flow
- ◎ Plenty of cardstock for your cards, tags, envelopes
- ◎ Lots of different color papers in a variety of weights and textures
- ◎ Simple tools such as scissors, tape, glue or other adhesives, paper cutters, punches, pens, paints, chalks
- ◎ Embossing items, rubberstamps, inks, etc.

▪▪▪▪▪▪▪▪▪▪▪▪▪▪▪▪▪▪▪▪▪▪▪▪▪

◉ A must have that will help you in finding just the right words are my books:

> The Ultimate Guide to the Perfect Word
> The Ultimate Guide to the Perfect Card
> Scrapping Expressions

◉ Idea books and your magazine collection

◉ Embellishments to your heart's content ranging from stickers of all shapes, sizes, textures, styles, glitter, jewels, ribbons, lace, eyelets, rub-ons, and the list goes on

◉ A computer, your favorite software and a color printer. There are a variety of programs available, some are graphic programs in general with special templates and then there are others specifically designed for card making

W ith supplies in
my hands
I use my love
of my art
To create a card for you
Straight from my heart

-Thena Smith

Let the creating begin—

Angels

- Grandmothers are angels in training
- Friends are angels on Earth
- A kind soul is inspired by loving friend
- Best friends are guardian angels in disguise
- Guardian Angels are touch our lives through friendships

Anniversary

- I Got You Babe
- Celebrate your love together
- Still crazy after all these years
- When a Man Loves a Woman
- Happy Anniversary—You did it
- Congratulations, job well done!
- You and Me Against The World
- Best Wishes on your happy occasion
- True love stories never have endings
- I love being married to my best friend!
- Still looking like newlyweds—young and in love
- Slow dancing together after all these years and loving it
- Before us lies eternity where our souls shall never part
- How far away the stars seem, how long ago was our first kiss

- Love reasons the heart and confounds the mind - LaTourelle

- More important than to be loved is that we do love

- I have found the one whom my soul loves -Song of Solomon

- I may grow old, but my heart will never grow tired of loving you

- Your love is a journey that began at forever and ends at never

- Love is two hearts beating as one. ____Years and more to come.

- Love is a circle without end, willing to give and ready to bend. -LaTourelle

- One hundred years will still be too few to be in love with you -LaTourelle

- Through the years it's better everyday, through the years God always made a way, through the years together we shall stay

- In time love comes full circle and is revealed in simple memories built by trust -LaTourelle

- Of all the joys in a long and happy life, there's none so precious as the love between husband and wife. May your years ahead be blessed with a wonderful journey.

- The love you share all these years makes this day special for all who know and love you

What greater thing is there for two human souls than to feel that they are joined together to strengthen each other in all labor, to minister to each other in all sorrows, to share with each other in all gladness, to be one with each other in the silent unspoken memories? —George Elliot

So Jacob served seven years to get Rachel, but they seemed like only a few to him because of his love for her. -Book of Genesis

Marriage is popular because it combines the maximum of temptation with the maximum of opportunity. Happy Anniversary! -George Bernard Shaw

You were made perfectly to be loved and surely I have loved you, the idea of you, my whole life long. -Elizabeth Barrett Browning

She is a winsome wee thing, She is a handsome wee thing, She is a lo'esome wee thing, this sweet wee wife o' mine. -Robert Burns

My darling love, they say the best is yet to be
So with thy heart, come grow old with me
Memories we shall build with blessings to treasure
Side by side, with a love that has no measure
-LaTourelle

First Year

One year of marriage together
Oh, how the time has flown
Days of joyous memories
Sometimes nights filled with storm
Through it all your love has grown
Giving you love to continue on

◉ Number one, the fun's just begun!

◉ One year... You made it!

◉ One year and still going strong

◉ The honeymoon continues

◉ Happy Anniversary and more to come

◉ Love is the beginning–Love is the end

◉ One year together and a zillion more

◉ You and me against the world

◉ Happy 1st Anniversary

For you on our anniversary my love–
The minute I heard my first love story
I started looking for you,
not knowing how blind that was.
Lovers don't finally meet somewhere.
They're in each other all along.
–Rumi

25 Years–Sterling Silver

- To a precious couple...Still shining with a special love. Happy 25th
- WOW! 25 years of wedded bliss–May your day be as special as you
- So many years together, you are still sterling as ever. May you shine on through.
- Through the years your love has endured
- The secret to your happy marriage must be those two little words–yes, dear!
- Twenty-five years of love–sent from God above

Thank you for the joys and sorrows
Looking forward to all our tomorrows

Love has kept you together– Love carries you through

In a marriage where love abides–
is a home shared side by side

- Twenty-five years and still shining like the stars
- When two souls meet...Love begins
- If ever there was love...It began and ended in you

Do you love me? Do you love me? After 25 years why do you ask me now?
-Fiddler on the Roof

50 Years of Golden Grace

- ◉ Only 50 years? And they said it wouldn't last. Awesome!

- ◉ Time has honored the essence of your love in every way

- ◉ Year after year you are more precious than gold

- ◉ Through the years, the good times and the bad, you've given all you had and love has brought you to this day

Happy days shared fill the treasure chest of life with very precious jewels called memories

Blessed with a marriage so laden with love. Strengthened and nurtured by God above. Memories and miracles built day by day. Touching many lives in a wonderful way. Today may this love come back to you. For all that you give and all that you do. Happy 50th Anniversary

-Linda LaTourelle

You are my first thought in the morning, my strength throughout the day, the words I whisper sweetly every evening when I pray

- ◉ Golden years filled with sunshine and rain
- ◉ Your love's seen you through again and again.
- ◉ Baby, it's been a sentimental journey with you all the way
- ◉ We celebrate your love today with praise to God who made the way

On this our golden wedding day
I pledge my love anew
Look at what our love doth say
We stood the ground and fought the fight
With love that was tested both day and night
Fifty years we have shared together
My darling know this, my love is forever
-LaTourelle

Golden like the sun
Aged like vintage wine
What a race you've run
Built with love divine
Memories yet untold
Blessings to behold
Precious and so rare
This life that you share
Happy 50th Anniversary
-LaTourelle

Golden years so filled with love
Sent to you from God above
Built with blessings and joy so rare
Oh what a treasure you two share
Many Blessings
-LaTourelle

As life grows older and so do we
May I have this dance with thee
Let us remember the night of glory
When once began our true love story
In my arms, as you waltz to music slow
Share in the memories of long ago
Years so full of joy and sorrow
Every day was a new tomorrow
Still here you are close by my side
Giving in faith, your love doth abide.
-Linda LaTourelle

When you are old and grey and full of sleep,
And nodding by the fire, take down this
book, and slowly read, and dream of the
soft look your eyes had once, and of their shadows
deep; how many loved your moments of glad grace,
And loved your beauty with love false or true,
But one man loved the pilgrim Soul in you,
And loved the sorrows of your changing face;
And bending down beside the glowing bars,
Murmur, a little sadly, how Love fled
And paced upon the mountains overhead
And hid his face amid a crowd of stars-Yeats

Did you never know, long ago,
how much you loved me, that
your love would never lessen
and never go? You were young then,
proud and fresh-hearted, you were too
young to know.   -Sara Teasdale

Happy olden days
Happy golden days
Fifty years so bright
Shine on forevermore

-LaTourelle

Love suffereth long, and is kind; Love envieth not; Love vaunteth not itself, is not puffed up, Doth not behave itself unseemly, seeketh not her own, is not easily provoked, thinketh no evil; rejoiceth not in iniquity, but rejoiceth in the truth; beareth all things, believeth all things, hopeth all things, endureth all things. Love never faileth...

Slow dancing together
after all these years and loving it

Many waters cannot quench love, neither can floods drown it.

-Song of Solomon

■■■■■■■■■■■■■■■■■■■■■■■■■■■■

If ever two were one, then surely we.
If ever man were loved by wife, then thee.
If ever wife was happy in a man,
Compare with me, ye woman, if you can.
I prize thy love more than whole mines of gold,
Or all the riches that the East doth hold.
My love is such that rivers cannot quench,
nor ought but love from thee, give recompense.
Thy love is such I can no way repay;
the heavens reward thee manifold, I pray.
The while we live, in love let's so persevere,
That when we live no more, we may live ever.
            -Anne Bradstreet

Apology

◉ Sorry, I'm a _____

◉ Guilty, Guilty, Guilty

◉ Forgive Me

◉ Forgive Me! My foot didn't fit in my mouth

◉ Did I say I was sorry?

◉ Forgiven?

◉ Did I say I was–WRONG? I was!

◉ How can I say I'm sorry?

◉ Let me count the ways

◉ How do you spell forgiveness?

◉ O.K. I blew it!

◉ Yep, it was MY fault–SORRY!

43

Baptism

Oh, what a wonderful blessed day
I know God hears every prayer I pray
For here you are honoring the Father and Son
By being baptized, my little one!
-Thena Smith ©

In my heart I have such joy
Over seeing the choice you made today
Such joy that could not be expressed
By any words that I might say

But I've stored in a very place
The awesome memories of this day
And be assured that for the rest of my life
They will be treasured and replayed
-Thena Smith ©

With joy in my heart
I celebrate this day with you
and always will be here for you
wherever you are and whatever you do
-Thena Smith ©

God loves you and cherishes you
for you are a treasure
His love for you exceeds
anything that can be measured
And this day is an answered prayer
that this moment in your life I could share.
May God bless you on this special day
and send Peace, love and joy your way.
-Thena Smith

Lord, look down from heaven above

touch this child with your wonderful love
Guide and protect this little one
throughout each hour until day is done
On your dedication to the Lord
Today we come together
to present you before the Lord
To give you back to Him
to love and adore

In my heart I have such joy
Over seeing the choice you made today
Such joy that could not be expressed
By any words that I might say
But I've stored in a very special place
The awesome memories of this day
And be assured that for the rest of my life
They will be treasured and replayed
-Thena Smith ©

With joy in my heart
I celebrate this day with you
And always will be here for you
Wherever you are and whatever you do
-Thena Smith ©

God loves you and cherishes you
For you are a treasure
His love for you exceeds
Anything that can be measured
And this day is an answered prayer
That this moment in your life I could share.
May God bless you on this special day
And send Peace, love and joy your way.
-Thena Smith ©

May joy and happiness fill your heart
As this new day has set you apart
With honor to our God above
May you feel His presence and His love.
-Thena Smith ©

Bar Mitzvah

- ◉ Mazel Tov on your Bar Mitzvah

- ◉ Wishing you a hearty Mazel Tov on your special day when you are called up to read from the Torah!

- ◉ With faith, there are no questions; without faith there are no answers -The Chofetz Chaim

- ◉ It is a tree of life to those who take hold of it, and those who support it will be enriched. - Proverbs 3:18

- ◉ In seeking wisdom the first step in silence, the second: listening, the third: remembering, the fourth: practicing, the fifth: teaching others. -Gabirol

Birth

A tiny little baby
So innocent and sweet
Will bring love and happiness
And make your family complete!

Baby~

Just another

WORD

For

Love!

God gave me His Love–God gave me children!

God creates a special gift
In His Heaven above
A gift that is full of joy and laughter

Full of sunshine and of Love

He places all of these wonderful things
Along with a tender heart
Inside a tiny baby girl
And blesses each precious part

He gives her tiny rosebud lips
And the softest baby skin

And just when she seems perfect
He touches her once again
Then he sends her to her family
Through her earthly mom to be
And she blesses all who love her

For all eternity!
I know the Father does these things
That only He could do
For there is no other way to explain

A blessing such as you!
-Thena Smith

■ ■

Birthday

Husband/Lover

To the Lover of my soul

Happy Birthday to My Hero in Love

To My Lord Handsome From Your Lady

Happy Birthday to the Love of My Life–From your Favorite Wife

Husband: H handsome U unique S smart B best A awesome N nice D dearest

This is the official "Husband of the Year" birthday award–You won! Happy Birthday!

Baby you're not getting older–you're approaching magnificent! Have a very Happy Birthday!

Some men are romantic and fly you to the moon
Others will help you and mow the yard in June
There are guys who love to dance all night
And wrap you in love and hold you so tight
But you my darling are someone so rare
Everything you do tells me you care.
So today on your birthday I pray for you
Blow out the candles, may wishes come true
Happy Birthday, Honey!
King for Today! May we crown you with blessings!
Happy Birthday to the one who rules our kingdom!

Honey, you are the best present you could ever give me.
So I didn't get you anything but me.
Don't you just love it?
No returns, perfect fit & looks great!
What more could you want?
Happy Birthday!

On Your Birthday, Dear
My gift to you on
this day is simply
my heart
my love
I give to you
forever and on
this special day
You are the only love of my life.
I Love You Happy Birthday

Love you Dear with all my heart
and hope for each other we will never part.
I think of you on this special day
and hope to show you in every way
that my love is deep and my love is true
I'm wishing a Happy Birthday to you!
-CC Milam

Dear Stephen,
May you have a wonderful day
as you reflect back on the memories
of birthdays past and realize
just how special you really are

May you know that you are a
blessing to me today and always.
May you thank the Lord for each
year that passes and thank Him
for giving you life.
May the Lord Bless you today
in a special way on your Birthday
-CC Milam

Thank You for Being a Wonderful Husband
Thank you Dear for your love and
the way you hold me close to you
Thank you Dear for the time you
spend with me and our beautiful children
Thank you Dear for the life that you
have worked so hard for- for all of us
Thank you Dear for being you and
for the joy you bring to your family and friends,
and for Being a Wonderful
Husband, Father, and Friend
-CC Milam

I would live in your love as the sea-grasses
live in the sea,
Borne up by each wave as it passes,
drawn down by each wave that recedes;
I would empty my soul as the dreams
that have gathered in me,
I would beat with your heart as it beats,
I would follow your soul as it leads.

-Sarah Teasdale

All perfect marriages are made up of cou-
ples who accept the fact that they have an
imperfect marriage. In dreams and in love
there are no impossibilities -Arnay

Keep me as the apple of the eye, hide
me under the shadow of thy wings

Wife/Lover

My Beautiful Lady
My Wonderful Queen
The Owner of my Heart

No other woman could be so much to so many,
You touch our lives in a special way
Giving, caring and always praying
What a blessing you bring to our life
Happy Birthday My Beautiful Wife

To My Loving Wife
Thank you for always loving me
even when I am hard to love
Thank you for always taking care
of the children God sent us from above
Thank you for all the little things you do
Thank you for just being you!
Happy Birthday
-August Jones

At times I cannot find the words to express
the love I feel for you and the happiness
you bring to me each new shiny day
and today I wish you a Happy Birthday
-CC Milam

Even though you do not hear me say those
three little words that mean so very much to you
I promise with all my heart that I do Love You
I pray your birthday is the best
-CC Milam

My Woman, My Woman, My Wife

On this birthday may all your wishes come true
May God hear every prayer spoken for you
You give to our lives so much love and care
You are precious to each of us beyond compare

A mother, a friend, the love of my life
I am so blessed to call you my wife
Happy Birthday, Darling
-CC Milam

Today is your day to celebrate
But today is my day to celebrate you
Happy Birthday to You!
Queen for a Day and My Life
Happy Birthday!

Father

I love you, Daddy
I'm so thankful you are my Father
To a Wonderful Man I Call My Father
To the King of his castle from his little Prince
May the Lord Bless You Today on Your Birthday
Chance made you my Father but love made you my Daddy
I know that you are not my real father but I'm thankful you are my Dad

Dear Daddy, I love you so much and will always be your little girl -CC Milam

Dear Dad, I'm so Thankful to the Lord that He Gave Me You as My Father

53

Thank you Dad for being such a wonderful role model for me to look up to. When I grow up I want to be a Godly man just like you. -August Jones

I was looking for the perfect card that really reflected something about the person you are, but I did not find any made with duct tape! -CC Milam

Growing up, I always felt so safe and protected by you. Thank you for always being there for me.
-CC Milam

Dear Dad,
You and I have been round the block and back again. And through it all we found home. A love that was born in that first breath, so many years ago, is the glue that has held with unwavering strength in each moment of struggle, and it the polished finish that makes my life shine. Your unfailing love as a father, has guided me over the hills and into the valleys and out again. Too often we missed the point that we are an awesome team because we were too busy being stubborn. But now as the years have moved on, it is with the deepest awe that I realize just how wise and good you really are. And in these fleeting moments of enlightenment it is my prayer that the memories of that little girl will flood your soul and you will once again feel love.
Love, Your #1

On Your Birthday I just wanted you to know that I love and respect you for the way you take such good care of me and your family. I am truly blessed to have you as my father. Blessing on Your Birthday!
-CC Milam

Dear Dad,
I know we have had our hard times and I feel that all of that is in the past. The love and respect I have for you now seems like it has always been and I know it will always last. -CC Milam

Dear Dad,
I loved going places with you as a little girl. You always made me feel like your little princess! -CC Milam

Dear Daddy,
I love you so much and when I get older, I'm going to marry you!
Love, Katie

The voice of parents is the voice of God's, for to their children, they are heaven's lieutenants

It's your birthday! Celebrate Make three wishes
Blow the candles Cut the cake Open the presents
Eat the cake Take a nap You've earned it
With all that work Happy Birthday!

Mother

- ◉ My Best Friend

- ◉ My Favorite Shopping Buddy

- ◉ I love you Mommy with all my heart

- ◉ You're the Best Mommy in the world!

- ◉ God could not be everywhere and therefore he made mothers

- ◉ All that I am, or hope to be, I owe to my angel mother -Abraham Lincoln

- ◉ Thank you Mom for being there for me and love me with all of your heart

A mother is she who can take the place of all others but whose place no one else can take -Cardinal Mermillod

Grown don't mean nothing to a mother. A child is a child. They get bigger, older, but grown. In my heart it don't mean a thing -Toni Morrison

I know I was not always an easy kid to raise but I hope you know that I love you and always have

It takes a special mother to make a house a home
To fill the rooms with laughter and never feel alone
I know I am so truly blessed to be the child of you
So on this day for mothers, I give my heart anew.
May God pour out his love on this Birthday
-LaTourelle

MY MOTHER

A pillar of strength, the pure meaning of Love
A Divine gift from our Lord up above
As gentle as rain on the petals of a rose
She'll kiss away fears and hug away woes
A doctor when tending a cold or a scrap
A chef when making cookies or frosting a cake
A tailor, a chauffeur, a fairy god mother at times
But never to busy for a child's nursery rhymes
A source of wisdom that comes from inside
A manager, a bookkeeper and a private tour guide
The one that knows just what to say
When a child is having a difficult day
The maker of dreams and the setter of goals
As a pile of laundry she sits and folds
When strange noises go bump in the night
It's her loving hand that turns on the light
All things to family she feels she must be
Although her family may not see
In our Lord's kingdom the one that will fare
Is the one we call Mother. No others compare!
                                        -Barbara K. Cox

What kind of memories does this poem
bring to mind about your own mother?

Another word for MOTHER is LOVE

A picture memory brings to me; I look across the years and see myself beside my mother's knee. I feel her gentle hand restrain my selfish moods, and know again a child's blind sense of wrong and pain. But wiser now, a man gray grown, my childhoods needs are better known. My mother's chastening love I own   -John Greenleaf Whittier

My mother gave me the best she had
She gave me all of her
And in the quietness of the night
Her prayers were lifted high for me
I must tell her just how wonderful she is
I must let her see that she is the best
Her love is the greatest gift
And I am so blessed to call her Mother

Child

If I could give you diamonds
for every hug you gave to me
If I could give you pearls for
The smiles you sent my way
If I could give you sapphires
For each kindness that you gave
Then your crown would be adorned
With gems of love more precious
Than all the kingdoms jewels
May you sparkle and shine
With these gifts from my heart
Happy Birthday

Daughter

Pretty Princess
My Little Blessing
My Little Princess
My Twinkle Toes
To My Loving Daughter
I'm thankful the Lord gave me you as a daughter to love
The Lord blessed my heart the day He gave me you

A Daughter is a joy bringer
A Daughter a heart warmer
A Daughter a memory maker
A Daughter is Love
A Daughter is You
Happy Birthday!

A Daughter is Love
A daughter is smile
A daughter is snuggles
A daughter is smart
A daughter is thoughtful
A daughter is giving
A daughter is honoring
A daughter is wonderful
A daughter is YOU!

You're the sparkle in my eyes
the twinkle in my toes
and the kiss on my heart
You are the gift I dreamed of
All of my life over and over
Now we celebrate your birthday
As you become a young woman
No matter how old you get
You will always be my little girl
Happy Birthday Dear Daughter
-LaTourelle

My Daughter
you are a beautiful person
I want you to know that
no matter what you do,
what you think,
or what you say
you will have my love forever.

Happy Birthday
-LaTourelle

Dear Daughter,
You have a way about you
that's definitely your own---
I see it in so many ways
Your thoughtfulness
Your intuition
Your smile
Your song
You are so special
I'm proud you are mine
I love You
Happy Birthday
-LaTourelle

In the thoughtful things you do
And the smile upon your face
You show your love so true
With your beauty and your grace
Happy Birthday
-LaTourelle

Whatever there is in my life that's right
Without a doubt you are the best
Your light shines and lifts the hearts
Of everyone that knows you
Daughter you are love
I am so very blessed
May your cup runneth over
On this your special day
-LaTourelle

The company of you
Is all my dreams come true
May this your day be special
And fill your heart with love
Happy Birthday Dear Daughter
-LaTourelle

A daughter is—
Your princess
Pink petunia
Tomboy in jeans
Dreamer and schemer
Lover of life
Precious and pretty
Perfectly sweet
The love of my life
-LaTourelle

What is a daughter?
She's a pleasure, a treasure, a comfort each day
Loving and sweet in her own special way
A daughter is you my beautiful child
For as long as I'm living my daughter you'll be
Happy Birthday
-LaTourelle

A daughter is love all wrapped up so sweet
She giggles with joy from way down to her feet
A treasure and comfort to delight every day
She fills up my life in her own special way
-LaTourelle

With each and every passing year
She grows much sweeter than before
Through every stage⬚ through every age,
You can't help but love her more.
She's charm and beauty
Love and delight
She's the one true love
That God did right
-Linda LaTourelle

Son

- What a Guy!
- Captain of my Heart
- You are my "Son" shine
- Thank Heaven for Little Boys
- Snips & Snails and Puppy Dog Tails
- That's my Boy!
- The Lord shined down upon on me the day He gave me you, a Son
- I'm so thankful the Lord gave me you as a son to love and cherish

My Little Prince
To My Son, I Love You
To My Wonderful Son
With Pride, To My Son
A reflection of your father

My Little Man
You're such a big boy!
You are the joy of our life.
Happy Birthday, Son!

Today is your day!
Let's celebrate the wonder of you–
Happy Birthday to our Son!
Only God Could Create a Little Boy

Look at that wonderful creature
That we call a little boy
Only God in Heaven above
Could create such a package of joy!

■ ■

Who would have thought of all of the things
That occupy a little boys mind?
If we were to look inside his head
What wonderful things would we find?

His imagination when let run free
Lets him wondrous things to see
And he finds joy in all manner of things
From rocket ships to tennis shoestrings!

He can love a puppy dog or a rat
With just as much ease
And when given the opportunity
A little boy loves to please.

Human beings can create
All manner of things to bring joy
But only a wonderful God of love
Could have created a little boy!
-Thena Smith

Happy Birthday to a guy who's smart,
charming, and absolutely gorgeous–
and I'd say so even if I WEREN'T your mom!
-Thena Smith

Dear Son,
If you ever wonder,
I will love you forever!

There is a special bond
Between a son and his mother
It has a tenderness and uniqueness
Unlike any other
From the time he is a baby
Held in those arms so loving
He knows this love is special
Sent from the Lord above him
As a toddler and youngster he knows
That his mom is special and tries
Always to be there to console him
When she hears his cries.
A teenager's love is so special
And even though it remains unspoken
There are special cords of love
That never can be broken.
But when he suddenly becomes a man
The emotions in his heart and soul
Respond as if on remote control
And he once again feels free to express
His love and warmth and tenderness.
The bond that has been dormant
For some of those teenage years
Brings joy to his mother's heart
And can reduce her to happy tears.
And when he chooses a wife to wed
He treats her with gentleness he learned from
The one who loved him like no other
His wonderful, loving and adored mother!
-Thena Smith

Sister

- A sister is a special kind of friend
  Sisters by chance, friends by choice.
- A little sister is someone to look up to.
- I loved you too much to be your friend, so God
  let me be your sister
- A sister is a bit of childhood that can never be lost
- There is no time like the old time, when you and I
  were young
- Sisters are different flowers from the same garden
- Chance made us sisters, hearts made us friends
- Giggles, secrets, sometimes tears, Sister and Friend
  through the years

Be kind to thy sister. Not many may know the
depths of sisterly love -Margaret Courtney

To have a loving relationship with a sister is not
simply to have a buddy or a confidant. It is to have
a soul mate for life -Victoria Secunda

The desire to be and have a sister is a primitive and
profound one that may have everything or nothing
to do with the family a woman is born to. It is a desire to know and be known by someone who shares
blood and body, history and dreams -Elizabeth Fisher

Our days sipping tea and
conversation shall never end
For though you're my sister, you
are always my friend

Dear Sister
Today on your birthday I pray
Health, wealth and happiness
And all your dreams come true
Happy Birthday

Happy Bearthday Sis
Remember when we used to play with our teddies
We dressed them all in their finest lace and silk
Together we sipped tea and ate the cookies mom
baked. Oh, what fun it was to talk and laugh and be
so silly. I dream often of the times we've shared, just
you and I. And I pray for the time when we shall do
it once more. My wish for you this birthday is that
you will find a quiet place to sit with a cup of tea
and in that special time you will remember love
and the special bond we share as sisters.

Secrets to whisper,
Memories to share,
A sister's love
Is forever near.

Much to the human heart's delight,
Love does indeed make all things right.
Through every joy, and any strife,
A sister is a friend for life!

S for sophisticated
I for intelligent
S for sweet
T for terrific
E for elegant
R for rare
All these things and more. Are everything that I
adore Happy Birthday, Sister

Sisters
Family
Friends
Forever
Birthday Blessings

Sister, You are the sweetness and love
Sent to me from heaven above
On your birthday may you know
My love is with you wherever you go
Happy Birthday

My Sister, My Friend
You are joy with out end
May your birthday be
The best it's ever been
And may you feel love
Coming down from above
Happy Birthday!
Sisters to talk
Laugh, sing and cry
God blessed us so
With a love til we die

Sisters are special
From young ones to old.
God gave me a sister
More precious than gold.

Enchanting and sweet
From your head to your feet
Touching my heart
My life is complete

You are my sister
You are my best friend
Oh how blessed
I have love without end

With a sister you share a common history
Of all that is, and what can be.
As childhood tears and innocent fears
Melt into memory over the years

Brother

- ◉ What are brothers for if not to share troubles and joys? Happy Birthday!
- ◉ A brother shares childhood memories and grown-up dreams.
- ◉ It was nice growing up with someone like you - someone to lean on, someone to count on someone to tell on!
- ◉ I'm smiling because you're my brother and I'm laughing cuz there's nothing you can do about it
- ◉ A brother is a little bit of childhood that can never be lost. Thanks for the memories.
- ◉ You taught me everything I really need to know
- ◉ The best thing about having a brother, I always had a friend

69

Grandsons

Grandsons are loved for many things,
for cheerful smiles and songs they sing
For bringing laughter and so much fun
Oh how we love you little one.

Filling us with pride
and giving so much more,
Grandson you're a blessing
We absolutely adore!
Happy Birthday with Love
-Thena Smith

Papa's Boy
Grandpa's Shadow

First in Our Heart-Our First Grandchild
Here is the most wonderful gift
That God could ever offer you.
Here is a special blessing.
Here is a dream come true.
Here is a bundle of sweetness
A source of joy in a crib
Here is innocence in a diaper
And love wearing a bib.
Here is hope for the future
That your arms can hold.
Here is your first grandchild
A treasure more precious than gold.
God knows of your homes and dreams
For it is He who placed them inside
Of the heart of yours that can hardly wait
To love, comfort, protect and guide!
-Thena Smith

Y ou are the joy in our heart and the apple of
our eye
A ray of sun in the morning and always our
sweetie pie.
You fill our lives with joy and gladness
And sometimes bring us a little sadness.
So on this special day we send to you a card full of
love for all the wonderful things you do.
May You Have a Wonderful Birthday
and Many Happy Days to Come
-CC Milam

Grandparents

Dear Grandpa,
Thank you for being
the best grandpa on earth!
I really mean it!
Happy Birthday
-CC Milam

Dear Papa,
I know I'm older now
but I only wish you
could bounce me
on your knee again
and throw me in the air
I love you, Papa
You will always have
a special place in my heart
Happy Birthday

Dear Grandpa,
I love to hear all the stories you tell me
and how I learn so much about you
and about life from them
I treasure them deep in my heart
where there is only room for
a special Grandpa like you!
Hope You Have a Happy Birthday
-CC Milam

On Your Special Day
One of my most favorite places to be,
Grandpa, is with you!
Because you're so special to me.
Happy Birthday
-CC Milam

Wishing You Happiness
Thank you could never say enough for
all that you do for me and all of our family
You are a wonderful treasure, Papa,
that is really rare and very priceless
We treasure you today on your Birthday
and on every day
-CC Milam

Papa,
I love how you wrap me in your arms with a great
big hug and tickle me to pieces down on the living
room rug. You pack me around with such pride and
joy and out of all that I play with, you are the best toy!
Happy Birthday Papa

Dear Grandma,
The best present in the world
Is when I get to spend time with you,
      grandma
You're sparkly and funny and smell good, too
I just hope you know how much I love you
May this little card I made for you
Always remind you how special you are
Happy Birthday
-LaTourelle

Grandma's are a kid's best friend
But I'm extra lucky because
My Grandma is my best, best friend
Forever and ever.
I hope you have a birthday as terrific
For you as you are to me.
I love you, Grandma
Happy Birthday

Niece

My sister gave to me
A daughter as sweet as she
With sparkling eyes
And giggles galore
What Aunt could ask
For anything more
Nieces are nice
Like sugar and spice
Nice and neat
A niece so sweet

Nephew

What a joy
My brother's boy
My brother in duplicate
God created brothers
And blessed us with
Their sons
What a blessing and joy
My brother's sweet boy

Aunt

To my special Aunt
I love you so much
Birthday Wishes
Sent with Hugs and Kisses

Happy Birthday with love
To a Special Lady in My Life
Thank you Aunt Hazel for being
the best aunt I have ever had
I love our special friendship and
all the time we spend together
Thank you for everything you have
taught me about life and myself
Thank you for all you have given
to me from your heart
May the Lord Bless You
Happy Birthday
-CC Milam

Uncle

Happy Birthday Uncle Jerry
Isn't it just great how much
talent, good looks, smarts, and
pride can come out of one family?
Sounds like you raised me pretty good, right?
-CC Milam

Happy Birthday Uncle Troy
Thank you for all that you do for me
and how you love me as your own
I love our special relationship
Thank you could never be enough
for such a wonderful man in my life
Thank you for your love
-CC Milam

Child and Teen

How does a car sound for your Birthday???
Honk! Honk! Well, Happy Birthday Anyway!
-CC Milam

Hope you have one bumper of a Birthday!
(Oh yeah! Cars have two bumpers! Sorry!)

So you really want to know who is on the $100 bill?
Didn't you learn that in history class?
Maybe you need to go look it up
after you have a Happy Birthday!
-CC Milam

Happy Birthday to One Cool Friend
Hope you have a great Birthday
-CC Milam

Look at you!
You are all grown up!
A teenager at last!
And I sit in amazement
that the time has gone so fast!
From the day I first held you
and wiped baby tears away
how could the years go so quickly
that brought us to this day!
I do not want to hold you back
I know that you must grow
But be you 2 or 20
Just know I love you so!
What has been happening?
Where have I been?
How did it happen
that you are turning ten!
-Thena Smith

I don't know how you grew up
without me seeing it going on
but suddenly there are candles
a cake, and the birthday song!!
-Thena Smith

What have I been doing?
Time flew swiftly by
My how you have grown
Into such a handsome guy

Friend

May your blessings be many
May your sorrows be few
May love be so special
Just like you
Happy Birthday Friend

A birthday is a good time to remember our friends.
Come to think of it, at our age, it's good to remember most anything at all! Birthday Blessings!

There's a miracle in our friendship
That dwells within my heart
Don't know when it happened
But I knew right from the start
The happiness you bring
Always gives my soul a lift
To me our special friendship
Is God's most perfect gift
Happy Birthday to You

Thank for being such an awesome friend!
You are so wonderful to me and you are
always there to listen when I need you
You really know how to cheer me up
when I am a little sad and blue
You have such a lovely smile that
always seems to brighten my day
Thank you for our friendship
Have a Happy Birthday
-CC Milam

Hope you have a Special Birthday
that is Special just like you!
Who would have thought that is this great big
world we would find each other???
You are the bestest friend I have ever had and
I hope we are friends forever!
Happy Birthday

Secret Pals

To My Secret Pal
May the Lord watch over you and keep
you in all that you to throughout your day
May He send His peace and comfort
and fill you with blessings in every way
You're in my prayers today and always
Your Secret Pal

May the Lord lead you and guide you
today and everyday and in every way!
Your Secret Pal

The Lord is good
The Lord is great
The Lord bless you
this day as we celebrate
Happy Birthday
From your Secret Pal

■■■■■■■■■■■■■■■■■■■■■■■■■■■■

Milestone Birthday
First

◉ The big ONE
◉ Bearly one year old
◉ One is Wonderful
◉ Happy First Birthday to Our Little Sweetie pie
◉ One year old and just begun

Kisses, Hugs, Diapers and Pins
A New Year of Fun and Joy Begins!
Come Celebrate Baby's First Birthday

Share the Joy
Let's Have Some Fun!
Our Little Baby
Is Turning One!

Watch me party
I'll be wearing my cake
It's my big ONE!

A tiny cake and lots of fun
Our little darling is turning one!

When God sends an angel to earth
We call this heavenly miracle "birth."
You grow sweeter with each passing day
How much you're loved, no words can say.
We hold your hand and you hold our heart
From the innermost tender part.
We watch you with love beyond what we've known
Amazed at what our love has sown.
This first year ends and we celebrate anew
The joy God brought us when He sent us you!
-Thena Smith

■■■■■■■■■■■■■■■■■■■■■■■■■■■■■■

My one year old daughter giggles with joy and sparkles with glee, she's sweetness and sunshine as she looks at me One moment with her And she'll steal your heart What a blessing she's been Right from the start Hugs and kisses Dresses and bows She's a miracle baby Every moment she grows   -Linda LaTourelle

Joyfully giggling and sparkling with glee,
my one year old daughter smiles softly at me
Just looking at her it's easy to see how she'll capture
your heart and bless you completely -LaTourelle

Thirteenth Birthday

◎ Welcome to the Teens
◎ Happy 13 [th] Birthday
◎ Teen Time
◎ You're a Teeny Now
◎ You're not a kid any more
◎ Look out world, Here I come!

Sixteenth Birthday

◎ Sweet Sixteen
◎ Sweet Little Sixteen
◎ No longer a child, barely a woman
◎ A Young Lady all Grown Up

◎ It's just that you've grown up before my very eyes
You've turned into the prettiest girl I've ever seen
Happy birthday sweet sixteen

La la la la la la la la la
◎ Happy birthday sweet sixteen

◎ So you are turning 16?
I'll be sure and stay off the sidewalks!

Sweet 16 and Never Been Kissed?
Please do not look for a prince by kissing frogs,
don't you know those things cause warts!
Hoppy Birthday!
-CC Milam

Fifteen years have come and gone
Your sixteenth year has begun to dawn
So sing with delight and dance with glee
For this is the day God gives to thee
Happy Birthday Sweet Sixteen

Eighteenth Birthday

Almost a Lady
Almost a Gentleman
Happy birthday to an almost adult

Have a great time turning 18!
Now your parents may let you stay out until 10pm!
Don't party to hardy!

So you are turning 18
What I wouldn't give to be 18 again
Love your body while you still got one
Those wrinkles are just around the corner!
Happy 18th Birthday
-CC Milam

You have your life ahead of you to go and
fulfill all the dreams you have dreamed and
to achieve all the goals you have planned for
Just remember us little people when you reach the top!
Happy 18th Birthday!
-CC Milam

Turning 18 today? Just look at you▢an adult before my eyes! My, the responsibilities you have to look forward to▢Like paying taxes this year, still paying high car insurance, and signing up for the military!
-CC Milam

Twenty-First Birthday

- ◉ Legal at last–have a blast
- ◉ Welcome to adult hood
- ◉ So you're just 3 in dog years!
- ◉ So you're mature now–Go get a job!
- ◉ With maturity comes responsibility, make wise choices. You're now an adult, do something useful like go take out the trash and clean your room!

Twenty-Ninth Birthday
29 Forever!
29 and barely holding on
29 AGAIN? Talk about recycling!
Happy Birthday

I'm 29 and you're not!
Have a great year!
Happy Birthday
-CC Milam

Really, turning 29 again?
You know you can not fool me with
those burn marks on your face–
What have I told you about trying to
iron out those wrinkles??
Happy Birthday and
throw that iron away!
-CC Milam

◉ Thirty

- ◉ Thirtysomething
- ◉ Thirty? Heeeeeeee!
- ◉ 30, now that is half of 60!
- ◉ A third of your life is over
- ◉ 30 is not so bad, you could be 40, 50, 60☐
- ◉ I would not say that you are old but all your favorite songs are on that classic rock station

I found the perfect solution for turning 30!
You see last year I had 29 put on my baseball shirt
Now I will be 29 forever!
Sorry number is taken you can't have it!
-CC Milam

Fifty

- ◉ Nifty Fifty
- ◉ Fifty is nifty
- ◉ After fifty it's patch, patch, patch
- ◉ Forty is the old age of youth; Fifty is the youth of old age
- ◉ 50 is not very old–if you're a tree!

I recently turned fifty, which is young for a tree, midlife for an elephant, and ancient for a quarter miler, who's son now says, "Dad, I just can't run the quarter with you anymore unless I bring something to read -Bill Cosby

Turning 50?

Your advanced for your age
Oak trees in their fifties
just start turning nutty.
Have a good one!
-CC Milam

■■■■■■■■■■■■■■■■■■■■■■■■■■■■

Over the Hill

- Ancient

- Jurassic–Prehistoric

- Blow torch, please!

- So many candles so little cake

- Lordy Lordy Look Who's Forty?

- The older the fiddler, the sweeter the tune

- Geezer, formerly known as "Stud Muffin"

- Born in the USA a loooooooong time ago

- You're not getting older, just think of it as more experienced

- Life is not measured by years, but anniversaries of the heart.

- Don't think of yourself as old, think of yourself as experienced.

- How old are you again? Tap your cane on the floor when I get close

- You know you're getting older when you know all the answers, but nobody asks you the questions anymore!

- At My Age, I've Seen It All, Done It All, and Heard It All–I Just Can't remember It All

Yes, it is getting hot in here and no,
I don't think it is you're hot flashes this time
From that blinding light,
I think it is you
Have a Hotty Birthday

Miscellaneous Birthday

- ◎ Let's Party!
- ◎ Older and Wiser
- ◎ Sparkling Wishes
- ◎ ____ And Holding
- ◎ Roaring Twenties
- ◎ You Take the Cake
- ◎ Let Them Eat Cake
- ◎ Oh, No! It's the Big -!
- ◎ Youth has no age-Picasso
- ◎ She's pretty, she's fine, but 39?
- ◎ You deserve nothing but the best
- ◎ This is your special day—for special you
- ◎ The first hundred years are the hardest.
- ◎ You deserve the best today□and always
- ◎ You were born an original-John Mason
- ◎ In youth we learn; in age we understand.
- ◎ May all your most magical wishes come true
- ◎ I'm not having hot flashes, just power surges
- ◎ Party, Cake, Ice Cream, Punch and YOU!
- ◎ Hey Diddle Diddle, You're older - a little!
- ◎ I am not a has-been, I am a will be -Lauren Bacall
- ◎ Smile, it's your birthday! Laugh, this is your present!

- Have a Fun-tastic Birthday! If you don't it's your own fault.

- Happy Birthday to Someone with Charm, Grace and Humor

- The Years tell us much that the Days never knew -Emerson

- There is nothing more the language of the heart than a wish

- So many candles–So little cake Don't forget the ice cream

- Grow old along with me! The best is yet to be - Robert Browning

- Happy Birthday–You're how old? Oh, I thought you were sisters!

- Birthdays are good for you The more you have, the longer you live

- It's your birthday, do stuff your not supposed to do. Happy Birthday!

- There was a star danced, and under that was I born -Shakespeare
  Our birthdays are feathers in the broad wing of time - Jean Paul Richter

- Youth comes but once in a lifetime -Henry Wadsworth Longfellow

- Nobility is not a birthright; it is defined by one's actions -Robin Hood

- Men are equal; it is not birth but virtue that makes the difference -Voltaire

- To me, old age is always fifteen years older than I am -Bernard M Baruch

- Birth may be a matter of a moment, but it is a unique one -Frederick Leboyer

- I have liked remembering almost as much as I have liked living -William Maxwell

- May your birthday be a day to remember and filled with joy to remember always

- Some guy's got it and some guy's don't, and you're definitely one of the Got-it's!

- You know you are getting old when the candles cost more than the cake-Bob Hope

- The advantage of being eighty years old is that one has many people to love. -Renoir

- May all your birthday dreams come true— especially the tall, dark and handsome one.

- Life is short–open your presents early! Have a great day and may all wishes come true.

- The dull, blunt needle of Time sews another button on a sadly worn pair of under drawers.

- For all the advances in medicine, there is still no cure for the common birthday - John Glenn

- Age does not make us childish, as some say; it finds us true children - Johann Wolfgang von Goethe

- I wanted to get you something totally impractical for your birthday, but then I realized you already have a husband.

- Real birthdays are not annual affairs. Real birthdays are the days when we have a new birth - Ralph Parle

- You say it's your birthday! Well, it's my birthday, too. No, not really, I just thought it might make you feel better - Nicocacola

- The secret of an enjoyable birthday can be found in achieving balance, cake, ice cream, cake, ice cream! Happy Birthday!

- The old believe everything; the middle-aged suspect everything; the young know everything -Wilde

- When you have loved as she has loved, you grow old beautifully -W. Somerset Mangham

- Middle age is when you've met so many people that every new person you meet reminds you of someone else -Ogden Nash

> Some people, no matter how old they get,
> never lose their beauty - they merely move
> it from their faces into their hearts.

The Land of Birthdays was simply beautiful. To begin with, there was always birthday weather there - brilliant sunshine, blue sky, and a nice little breeze. The trees were always green, and there were always daisies and buttercups growing in the fields. -Enid Blyton

You can take no credit for
beauty at sixteen. But if you are
beautiful at sixty, it will be
your soul's own doing.

We will not speak of years tonight
For what have years to bring but
larger floods of love and light,
and sweeter songs to sing? -Oliver W Holmes

May the dreams you hold dearest,
Be those, which come true,
The kindness you spread,
Keep returning to you.

May your day be filled with blessings,
like the sun that lights the sky,
And may you always have the courage
to spread your wings and fly!

!If wrinkles must be written on our brows,
let them not be written upon the heart.
The spirit should never grow old. -Garfield

Belated Birthday

◎ I didn't forget–I was delayed.

◎ I'm not late–I'm early...in another time zone

◎ Happy Birthday from a little bit behind–Me!

◎ You had what? A Birthday? Well, golly–I plum
fergot!

◎ Oh I sent you this card late on purpose! I was
just prolonging your birthday!

◎ Sure it's late, but that's just to catch you off-
guard! Happy Belated Birthday!

◉ Heard you had a great birthday–just heard it a little late! Hope it was great fun–like you!

◉ I'm sorry I missed your birthday–I misplaced my mind somewhere! Belated blessings!

◉ Oops–I missed it! Hope it was a day to remember! Just like you! Happy Birthday

◉ My motto is put off today what you can do tomorrow. I did! Happy Birthday, hope it was great!

◉ You look just too young to have had another birthday! And I look so bad to have missed it!

◉ I didn't forget your birthday–I just wanted to help extend the celebration!

◉ Late is such a ugly word, Let's just say this card is promptness challenged!

◉ Of course I remembered it was your birthday...I just forgot the date.

◉ Oh, my goodness, me oh, my! I let your birthday slip right by!

Pastors

◉ Shepherd of the Flock

◉ When I look into your eyes I see the love that God has given me two hands clasped in prayer can do more than a hundred working

◉ Prayer is exhaling the spirit of man and inhaling the spirit of God -Edwin Keble

◉ Who rises from prayer a better man, his prayer is answered -George Meredith

Dear Pastor
Thank you for being such a blessing to our family
You have given to our family in so many ways
through your time, your prayers, and your heart
Thank you for being such a wonderful man of God
May the Lord Abundantly Bless you
Happy Birthday

You guide us with your loving hand
And comfort us with prayer
We thank you for such dedication
Dear Pastor you are so rare
-LaTourelle

When God looks down upon his church
And hears your words and watches your care
He sees in you a man that longs to be like Jesus
What a blessing you are to us as you lead us
To a deeper understanding of what real love is
Thank you for your loving example
And for keeping us in your prayers
May you be blessed abundantly
Happy Birthday (or other occasion)
-Linda LaTourelle

Dear Pastor
May the Lord bless you and restore you
May He give you comfort and rest
May He guide you in His path
May He give you strength and encouragement
May He fill your life with peace and joy
May You Have a Happy Birthday

Blessings

May you always have-
Walls for the winds,
A roof for the rain,
Tea beside the fire,
Laughter to cheery you,
Those you love near you,
And all that your heart may desire

Let me walk beside you
in sunlight or in rain
Let me share your joy
And your times of pain

A blessing is a gift so full of grace
Welcomed with love no matter the place
Thank you my love for all that you are
My treasure, my love, a heavenly star

May memory open the heart's door wide
And make you a child at your mother's side
And may you feel her love around you
As happy memories surround you!

The Lord shall bless thee and keep thee.
The Lord make his face to shine upon thee and be
gracious unto thee.
The Lord lift up his countenance upon thee and
give thee peace.
And they shall put my name upon the children of
Israel and I will bless thee.
-Numbers 6:24-27 KJV

Bon Voyage

Flyin' high
Many miles
Happy day
Let's go play
Forecast-Sunny skies
Having fun now
Have the time of your life
A day at the beach is sand-tastic
Just plane fun

Wherever you go, whatever you do,
may your guardian angel watch over you

Traveling down that long lonesome highway?
You're not alone God's in the driver's seat!

Bridal Shower

Let's Shower the Bride-to-be!
A cord of three is not easily broken
Your Invited to a Bridal Shower

Today is the day she prepares for the future
As she is surrounded by family and friends
They are helping her with gifts for her house
And with love where a home begins
 May the Lord Richly Bless You
Today and In the Years to Come
-CC Milam

In just a few more days,
She will gladly say, "I do"
In a white satin gown with something
Borrowed and something blue
-CC Milam

Cardmaking

Cardmakers write with love
Cardmaking Princess
Handmade with love
Beware, Cardmaker On Duty
Make a card–Save a tree
I'd rather be making cards
Card makers never die, they just fold-up
Cardmakers are Creative, Classy and Cute
Cardmaking is my life, everything else is work
Cardmakers give the gift that keeps on giving
Silly, sassy, sentimental–cardmakers say it superbly
Cardmaking is my passion. But chocolate comes in a
very close second!

If you need a poem
And you don't know where to start
Just put your pencil to the page
And write what's in your heart.
The words don't have to rhyme
And maybe they seem odd
But just write what's in your heart
And leave the rest to God.
For if he gives you the nudge to write
To console a hurting friend
Just put your pencil to the page
And the words the Lord will send.
Don't worry about what people think
About your verse or you
For God knows someone who needs
Just that word from you!
-Thena Smith

Celebrations

- ◉ Cheers
- ◉ Celebrate!
- ◉ Having a Party
- ◉ Here's to You
- ◉ The Joy of You
- ◉ A Night to Remember
- ◉ A Time to Celebrate
- ◉ Celebrate Good Times

Chanukah

Today we light the Chanukah menorah
With eight branches to glow so bright
And for eight days we do this
Adding one new candle each night.

We will spin the Dreidle
Our top that is such fun.
We will have good things to eat
And enjoy each and every one.

Latkes and sufganiyot
Are among our special treats
But Chanukah is a special celebration
Of much more than just good eats.
-Thena Smith

Children

There is a garden in every childhood,
an enchanted place where colors are brighter,
the air softer, and the morning more fragrant than
ever again
-Elizabeth Lawrence

95

Chocolate

- Chocolate–Need I say more?
- Chocolate solves everything!
- Friends are the chocolate chips of life
- Sisters & chocolate make life bearable
- I love you as much as chocolate itself!
- Not enough time and too little chocolate!
- Forget love! I'd rather fall in chocolate!

Christmas

- He is the King of Kings and Lord of Lords
- When you wish upon a star–Choose Jesus
- Hang a shining star upon the highest bow
- May the joy of the holidays fill your hearts
- Silent Night, Peace on Earth and With Yours
- God grant you the light in Christmas, which is faith
- Have a twinkle, jingle, ringy ding ding Christmas
- Don't go under the mistletoe with anyone else but me
- To My Santa–from the Mrs.
- Love was born on Christmas day
- Hark! The Herald Angels Sing
- Wishing you a joy filled Christmas
- Merry Wishes–Santa's Kisses
- Oh, Little town of Bethlehem
- Ring the bells, its Christmas!
- Wishing you a holiday of love
- Peace on earth□goodwill to you all
- Believe and you will find Christmas

Our hearts grow tender with childhood memories and love of kindred, and we are better throughout the year for having, in spirit, become a child again at Christmastime.
-Laura Ingalls Wilder

96

The rooms were very still while the pages were softly turned and the winter sunshine crept in to touch the bright heads and serious faces with a Christmas greeting -Louisa May Alcott

The merry family gatherings—
The old, the very young;
The strangely lovely way they harmonize in carols sung. For Christmas is tradition time—
Traditions that recall
The precious memories down the years,
The sameness of them all
-Marshal

Christmas Eve was a night of song that wrapped itself about you like a shawl but it warmed more than your body it warmed your heart, filled it, too, with a melody that would last forever -Aldrich

Somehow, not only for Christmas, But all the long year through, The joy that you give to others, Is the joy that comes back to you -Whittier

Let us get back our childlike faith again -Grace Noll Crowell

Come sit at my table and share with me, warm gingerbread cookies and cinnamon tea, just you and me!

■■■■■■■■■■■■■■■■■■■■■■■■■■■■■

CHRISTMAS IN OTHER LANGUAGES

Afrikander - Een Plesierige Kerfees
Argentine - Feliz Navidad
Armenian - Shenoraavor Nor Dari yev Pari Gaghand
Brazilian - Boas Festas e Feliz Ano Novo
Chinese - (Mandarin) Kung His Hsin Nien bing Chu Shen Tan
Danish - Gldelig Jul
Dutch - Vrolijk Kerstfeest en een Gelukkig Nieuwjaar!
English - Merry Christmas
Finnish - Hauskaa joulua
French - Joyeux Noel
German - Froeliche Weihnachten
Greek - Kala Christouyenna!
Hawaiian - Mele Kalikimaka me ka Hauoli Makahiki ho
Hebrew - Mo'adim Lesimkha Chena tova
Hungarian - Kellemes Karacsonyi unnepeket
Icelandic - Gledileg Jol
Indonesian - Selamat Hari Natal
Iraqi - Idah Saidan Wa Sanah Jadidah
Irish - Nodlaig mhaith chugnat
Italian - Buone Feste Natalizie
Japanese - Kurisumasu Omedeto
Norwegian - God Jul Og Godt Nytt Aar
Philippines - Maligayang Pasko
Polish - Wesolych Swiat Bozego Narodzenia
Portuguese - Boas Festas
Romanian - Sarbatori vesele
Russian - Pozdrevlyayu s prazdnikom Rozhdestva is Novim
Samoan - Maunia Le Kilisimasi ma Le Tausaga Fou
Scottish - Nollaig Chridheil agus Bliadhna Mhath Ur
Serb-Croatian - Sretam Bozic Vesela Nova Godina
Spanish - Feliz Navidad
Swedish - God Jul and (Och) Ett Gott Nytt Ar
Vietnamese - Chu'c Mu`ng Giang Sinh
Welsh - Nadolig Llawen
Yugoslavian - Cestitamo Bozic

Beneath a shining star,
Upon a Silent night,
within a lowly stable
the gift of love was born
-Sherry Moss

Let there be
JOY in our laughter,
LOVE in our laughter,
HOPE in our eyes,
PEACE in our hearts
-Sherry Moss

Candles and stars &
Christmas tree lights,
Twinkle and glow
In the velvet night

God bless the master of this house,
The mistress also,
And all the little children,
That round the table go,
And all your kin and kinsmen
Than dwell both far and near;
I wish you a Merry Christmas
And a Happy New Year
-Traditional from England

ON MY CHRISTMAS TREE

Hangs a picture of Grandma and me
Her smile's so sweet
And her heart's so big
She loves to bake bread and cookies
And fills up my tummy with treats
Every night I thank the Lord
For giving her to me.

Are you going home for Christmas? Have you written you'll
be there? Going home to kiss the mother and to show her
that you care? Going home to greet the father in a way to
make him glad? If you're not I hope there'll never come a
time you'll wish you had. Just sit down and write a letter—it
will make their heartstrings hum with a tune of perfect gladness—if you'll tell them that you'll come. -Edgar Guest

Christmas comes but once a year
May this card bring joy and cheer
Hope your days are cheery and bright
Lift your hearts look up tonight

The holy star shines bright for us,
that we may find the love of Christmas

99

Dear Santa Letters

Dear Santa,
Is true that you have jelly in your belly?
Love, Nattie

Dear Santa,
I promise I've been good and if you thought I haven't, it was all my sister's fault
Love, Katelyn

Dear Santa,
You sure do look like my Grandpa, ut that's o.k., because he's the best guy. I love him and I love you, too. Could you bring me a saddle for the pony Grandpa made me that he thinks I don't know about. I'll be having sweet dreams until you come.
Giddy up and fly, Love, Koby

Dear Santa,
Did you know why Christmas is so special? Well, God gave me the best present of all, His son, Jesus. I know you can't top that, but did you get my list of wishes?
I'll be Your little man, Alex

Dear Santa,
Mom says I've been naughty, but you know I'm really nice. Oh, what's a girl to do? We just like to figure stuff out by ourselves. We don't mean to get into trouble, it just happens. Anyway, I'm thanking you ahead of time for coming to my house. You will, won't you?
Love, Cheryln

Dear Santa,
Umm, I have to tell the truth, I really haven't been that good, but I'll bake you some really big cookies. Oh, and forget the milk, I'm leaving you hot chocolate, so you can stay warm. Does this help?
Your friend, Olivia

■ ■

Dear Santa,
Girls just wanna have fun. And more fun and more fun.
Sometimes we just get carried away and then mom gets mad.
I guess she's too old to see we were just playing. But you
know don't you? Can't wait to see you. Maybe you could tell
her to pretend she didn't see us.
Hugs and Cookies, Candace

Dear Santa,
I just want you to know that I don't really need anything, so
if you could just take my presents to someone who doesn't get
much for Christmas, that would be the best present ever.
Knowing that somewhere some kid is happy on Christmas
morning is the biggest blessing.
Your friend, Kasara

Dear Santa,
Did anyone ever tell you that red is my favorite color? You
wear it so well. But that beard! Has anyone ever asked if they
could give you a makeover? Well, I'm learning all this new
stuff watching my mom do hairstyles on her customers. I bet
I could make you look totally cool. Just think about it,
maybe that could be my Christmas present to you. Oh, and
this year, instead of the usual milk and cookies—I'm giving
you gourmet peanut butter and jelly sandwiches and some
mocha java. Maybe it'll help you stay awake better. I saw the
recipes on that Good Thing show I watch. Hope you like it.
To the new you,
Hannah

Dear Virginia,
Yes, there is a Santa Claus.
Thank you for writing.
Merry Christmas,
The Sun

101

TWAS THE DAY BEFORE CHRISTMAS

It was the day before Christmas while at the store
The isles were crowded making shopping a chore
When a man started yelling right at my face
It seemed to upset him, I got his parking place

The clerk said," Merry Christmas," but I could feel
That the words she were saying weren't so real
Out of money, but still room in Santa's sack
I pulled out my plastic and continued to pack

There was pushing, shoving and rude dirty looks
The warning on T.V. said," Look out for crooks,"
Our children must have the most on the block
It made no difference, if we went into hock

Then on a shelf that was almost picked clean
There all alone stood a Nativity Scene
I looked at baby Jesus from the land of Galilee
There were no lights, decorations or even a tree

I thought of the wise men who traveled so far
To find the baby Saviour they followed a star
There in a manger in a stable so cold
Was the greatest story that was ever told

I remembered our Lord, The King of all kings
I thought of Christmas and what it really means
I looked around at the faces wanting more
Put my cards in my pocket and walked out the door.
                    -Barbara K. Cox

■■■■■■■■■■■■■■■■■■■■■■■■■■■■■■■■

Merry Christmas to all and to all a goodnight!

FAMILY CHRISTMAS TREE

I opened the box marked Christmas
Getting ready to trim the tree
As I took each ornament out
I held an old memory

There's a Santa that belonged to Father
When he was a just a little boy
And snowflakes made by Grandma
That fill the room with joy

Bright red bows and silver bells
That take their place on the side
As children's pictures in egg carton frames
Will be displayed right in front with pride

And in the box is Mother's Angel
That will look down from atop the tree
In her hands, she holds a candle
For all the world to see

Now with each year that passes
They become more precious to me
Decorations passed down from generations
Filled with our family history

I will pass the box marked Christmas
To my children, for their legacy
A reminder our spirits are with them
On their family Christmas tree!
-Barbara K. Cox

THE CHRISTMAS MESSAGE

There's a chill in the air and the sweet smell of pine
Friends coming together it's Christmas time
Children playing with sleds on the new fallen snow
Toys in store windows have their eyes all aglow
Chapel bells ringing from the old town square
Decorations on main street being put up with care
Christmas shoppers beginning to fill the malls
Where trees are adorned with garland and balls
Out Christmas shopping I spotted a sign
"Santa's workshop" with children waiting in line
I walked up much closer so that I could hear
What the children wanted from Santa this year
When from in line I saw a young lad
By the look on his face, he was troubled and sad
I walked nearer yet so that I could see
As he took his turn upon Santa's knee
Santa, I don't want any toys under the tree
All I want is my Daddy here with Mommy and me
It's been so long since he's been gone
When he left the grass was still green on the lawn
You see, we're in the Military and he had to go
And Mommy and I miss him more than you know
When I'm in bed and she thinks I'm asleep
She reads over his letters and starts to weep

But if you can't do it Santa, I'll understand
Since Daddy's been gone, I'm Mom's little man
As you deliver your presents give a message from me
We gave up Christmas with Daddy so children stay free.

-Barbara K. Cox

A CHRISTMAS INVITATION

You are cordially invited to a Birthday Party of Love
GUEST OF HONOR: Jesus Christ
DATE: Today or any day–Traditionally, December 25
TIME: Now is the time
PLACE: In your heart–He'll meet you there,
just ask Him to come in
RSVP: He must know ahead, so He can reserve a spot
for you at the table and in His Invitation Book
PARTY GIVEN BY: His Children. Hope To See–You
There! Let us rejoice and be glad!
Please invite your friends to come
and join in the celebration of Love
Revelation 19:7-9

Confirmation

May joy and happiness fill your heart
And may this day set you apart
With honor to our God above
May you feel His presence and His love
-Thena Smith

On this day as you seek to grow
And more about your God to know
May you hear His voice as He speaks to you
And to His commandments always be true.

Easter

He is Risen! Hallelujah!
Our Risen Lord and Savior
Hoppin' Down the Bunny Trail
You're no bunny 'til somebody loves you
May your treasure this Easter be a new life in Jesus
Jesus died for you so you may have life eternal

■ ■

In your Easter bonnet with all the frills upon it,
You'll be the grandest lady in the Easter Parade
But he was wounded for our transgressions,
he was bruised for our iniquities:
the chastisement of our peace was upon him;
and with his stripes we are healed -Isaiah 53:5

Our Lord has written
the promise of the resurrection
not in books alone,
but in every leaf in springtime. -Martin Luther

Tomb, thou shalt not hold Him longer;
Death is strong, but Life is stronger;
Faith and Hope triumphant say
Christ will rise on Easter Day. -Phillips Brooks

Easter is God's promise that He loves us one and all,
He gave His Son to live for us and bids us hear him call.

Encouragement
Go Forth and Prosper
These are the moments.
Be the victor, not the victim
Smile! It confuses people!
Chocolate solves everything!
Listen to what your heart is saying
You mean the world to someone ME!
Some things are only felt with the heart
A smile is a curve that sets things straight
Some pursue happiness, others create it
Imagination is the soul within -LaTourelle
Simple pleasures are priceless treasures.

May God grant you always
A sunbeam to warm you,
A moonbeam to guide you,
A sheltering angel,
so nothing can harm you
May your troubles be few
And your blessings be more
And nothing but happiness
Come through your door

Let me be your hope when life seems desperate
Let me be your laughter crying through the tears
Let me be the touch that will lift your spirits
Let me be the heart beating strong for you
Let me be your strength when you're feeling weak
Let me be everything to you
-Linda LaTourelle

Take time to laugh. It is the music of the soul
Whenever you feel lonely, a special angel drops in for tea
The soul would have no rainbow, if the eyes had no tears
No bird soars too high if he soars with his own wings

Be who you are and say what you feel
Because those who mind don't matter,
And those who matter don't mind.
-Dr. Seuss

Take a leap of faith
and watch what God can do

There are times when your worries
seem more than you can bear
Kneel down, close your eyes
Give it to God, he'll answer your prayer

I know that times are difficult
And life seems very hard
But in the midst of trials
Our strength is so revealed
A hand is there to hold you
With a love like none before
So trust and seek the wisdom
That will guide you ever on
-LaTourelle

You are the strength when the world is weak
You are the light when the world is dark
You are the joy when the sorrow is heavy
You are the love when there is no more
-LaTourelle

I am here to lift you up
To brighten all your days
My arms will gladly hold you
And wipe your tears away
-LaTourelle

The highest reward for a person's toil
is not what they get for it, but what
they become because of it   -Ruskin

The longest journey is the journey inward

To serve God, to laugh and cry and laugh in spite of it all, to have your priorities in order, to hold a child's heart with love and their hand with encouragement, to learn from the old and give more than you took, to appreciate the touch of the Master's hand, to see the best in others by being the best in yourself, to serve others, to give all you can from your heart not just your bank account, to pray daily, to live contentedly, to keep the faith, to fight the fight and walk the walk, to leave the world a better place than you see it around you, to know that you have made a difference in at least one life, that my friend is honor, integrity, trust, success, the purpose in a life well-lived   -Linda LaTourelle ©2004

The greatest thing in this world is not so much where we are, but in what direction we are moving -Oliver Holmes

Today when you need a friend to simply hold your hand, close your eyes and feel my presence enfolding you with love -LaTourelle

- ◎ Just think, you're here not by chance, but by God's choosing to fulfill His special purpose

- ◎ Do not wish to be anything but what you are, and try to be that perfectly -St. Francis de Sales

- ◎ Never give up, for that is just the place and time that the tide will turn. -Harriet Beecher Stowe

- ◎ To achieve the impossible, it is precisely the unthinkable that must be thought. -Tom Robbins

You must do the thing you think you cannot do
–Eleanor Roosevelt

Nothing is beneath you if it is in the direction of your life -Ralph Waldo Emerson

109

■■■■■■■■■■■■■■■■■■■■■■■■■■■

Engagement

Engaged in Love

Once Upon a Time

Let the journey begin

Happy Coming Wedding

Young love, sweet love

We've only just begun

The best is yet to come

Let the best begin tonight

Marriage began in a garden

You are my first, my last, my all

Congratulations on this special day

May this be the beginning of a lifetime of love

Tonight is the beginning of your home and family

Diamonds are a girl's best friend and what a gem you have chosen

Father's Day

1 Dad

Hop on Pop

Fathers are a work of heart

My Daddy hung the moon

My Heart belongs to Daddy

No One Can Fill Your Shoes

Our Dad has a heart of gold

Daddy you're the best

He's my Dad!

Oh how I love Daddy!

DAD'S TOOLS
Dependability
Faith in God
Dedication
Stability
Fairness
Pride
Love

Thank you
for being there
through the years
to listen
to cheer me on
to support me
To love me,
Happy Father's Day

Thanks
for giving me the
best things in life–
your time, your
care, your love.
Happy Father's Day

Of all the gifts I've
ever received,
The gift I cherish
most is YOU.
Happy Father's Day
-LaTourelle

You're so great
I couldn't have picked
A better dad if I tried
Happy Dad's Day
I want to share the
Best in me with others
Because it's came
from you
Thank you for
unconditional love
Everyday of my life
You are the best Father
A child could
hope for
Happy Father's Day

A father is neither an anchor to hold us back, nor a sail to take us there, but a guiding light whose love shows us the way

If happy thoughts were flowers I would send you a bouquet

Tip toe through the tulips with me

Tis sweet perfume of lilacs scenting the morning breeze
As melodious robin redbreast awakens me with his call
The roses wind with laziness and such a gentle ease
Oh what a wonderful blessing—the wonder of it all
-LaTourelle

Think of all the beauty around you and be happy

People will forget what you said, will forget what you did, but will never forget how you made them feel.

The best portion of a good man's life is his little nameless, unremembered acts of kindness and of love -Wordsworth

Fourth of July

We hold these truths to be self evident,
that all men are created equal -Thomas Jefferson

I know not what course others may take,
but as for me, give me liberty or give me death
-Patrick Henry

Our flag is red, white and blue,
but America is a rainbow
Red and yellow, black and white -
we are precious in His sight

United we stand, forever in freedom it waves
God Bless America

Friends

I never came to you, my friend,
and went away without
some new enrichment of the heart;
More faith and less of doubt -Grace Cowell

'Stay' is a charming word in a friend's vocabulary
-Louisa May Alcott

Knowing that someone cares
and holds us close in their prayers
Knowing that we're understood
Makes everyday living feel wonderfully good
-LaTourelle
I wish for you a sunny day
with skies so blue
and time to pray
I wish for you a song-filled heart
a peace so delightful
with love from the start
-LaTourelle

By these words May you always know
That my love is with you wherever you go
-LaTourelle

Tweedle dee and tweedle dum
Love to play with hugs and fun
Laughter and smiles the whole day through
Oh what a joy when shared by two
-LaTourelle

I wish for you a sunrise
So spectacular to view
I wish for you a sunset
As magnificent as you
-LaTourelle

Oh what a beautiful face
Filled with such beauty and grace
Your smile is divine
Your love so sublime
Thank you for giving to me
All that I ever did need
-LaTourelle

It's amazingly clear
There's nothing so dear
As a friend by your side
Along for the ride

When I count my many blessings
It isn't hard to see
The greatest gift I have
Is the love you have for me
-LaTourelle

Have you ever seen a sunset grand, been caressed by a baby's hand, gleaned the wisdom from an old man's face, experienced the freedom of immeasurable grace. Then you, my friend, are blessed so much. Thanks to the love of your Master's touch. So know that today and forever more
His awesome power will carry you far
Don't welcome worry as an old friend

Give it up daily, for joy without end
-LaTourelle

When Prayers Go Up - Blessings Come Down
Large pink petal roses
with long green stems,
White daisy flowers
all neat and trimmed,
A gift of love-
sent from a friend.
-CC Milam

May the road rise to meet you
May the wind be always at your back
May the sun shine warm upon your face
May the rains fall soft upon your fields
And until we meet again,
May God hold you in the
hollow of His hand

I love you dearly and am so blessed
to call you friend! -LaTourelle
My love doth hold you close at heart, in friendship
dear right from the start -LaTourelle

Your gentleness made you my friend
Your compassion made you my confidant
and your strength in adversity made you my hero

I count myself in nothing else so happy, as in a soul
rememb'ring my good friends -William Shakespeare

A Friend Loves at all Times

OLD FRIENDS

Wandering back through the rivers of time
As special memories flood my mind
People and places that once meant so much
Now we rarely even keep in touch
We went to your house you came to our home
So long ago, before the children were grown
We went out for dinner, even danced a few
Oh, the secrets we shared between me and you
I recently walked through the old neighborhood
The houses now seemed just stucco and wood
New families now making their own memories
Raising their children and sowing their seeds
Although we have parted and gone our own ways
I sometimes journey back to those familiar days
To you my friends, I'll lift my glass
As long as there's memories, friendships will last!
-Barbara K. Cox

There are good ships, wood ships
And ships that sail the sea
But the best ships are friendships,
and may we always be

And in the sweetness of friendship
let there be laughter, and sharing of pleasures.
And let there be no purpose in friendship
save the deepening of the spirit.
-Kahil Gibran

When one is helping another both are strong
Thank you for giving me strength
And a friendship I cherish
I Love You

■■■■■■■■■■■■■■■■■■■■■■■■■■■■■

Fun

Shopping–Need I say more?
Wanna have fun?
Fun, Fun, Fun–Let's Go!
Play? Is there anything else?

Gardeners

- ◎ Time began in a Garden
- ◎ Flowers of true friendship never fade
- ◎ One is never nearer to God's heart than in a garden
- ◎ Friends are the flowers of heaven
- ◎ If friends were flowers, I'd pick you
- ◎ Friends are flowers in the garden of life
- ◎ Hearts that love are always in bloom
- ◎ My world without you for a friend would be like a garden full of weeds
- ◎ Your love is the nurturing touch
- ◎ Your seeds of love have changed my life–Thanks

Get Well

Hope is the thing with feathers
That perches in the soul
And sings the tune without the words
And never stops - at all
And sweetest - in the Gale - is heard
And sore must be the storm
That could abash the little Bird
That keeps so many warm
I've heard it in the chilliest land
And on the strangest Sea
Yet, never, in Extremity
It asked a crumb - of Me

-Emily Dickinson

You mean a lot to me
So does your health
and happiness
Get Well Soon

A Prayer for Your Recovery
Was sent Heavenward today
I trusted God to guide me
In just how I ought to pray.
So I am trusting that He heard me
And you will soon be feeling fine
And we will rejoice together
Dearest friend of mine!
-Thena Smith

With the warmest of wishes
This just comes to say
Hope that you're feeling
Much better today

So you're sick
Look on the bright side
Now you finally
have a reason
to whine and complain!
Get Well Soon

Let there be sunshine
to chase the clouds away
Kind thoughts to cheer you
and brighten your day

Know that someone cares
and is keeping you in their prayers

He who has health has hope, but he who
has hope has everything

Being in the hospital
is a downer
but look on
the bright side
you get breakfast in bed!
Cheery Day!

Get Well Soon
Sorry you're not
feeling your best
Sure hope you're
better soon!
Best Wishes

I wish for you a sunny day
with skies so blue and time to pray
I wish for you a song-filled heart,
a peace so delightful
with love from the start

I've got the perfect over-the-counter prescription to make you feel better real quick—Chocolate! It will do the trick every time.

It won't be long before you're all better and back to being your same old self again—enjoy this rest while it lasts!

Sending hugs and kisses and really big get well wishes
Wishing you a speedy recovery and happy days!

Hope you feel
like your
wonderful self again
very soon
Get Well Quick!

Girls

Diva Sisters

Best Friends Forever

Girlfriends are forever friends

You're not just my sister—you're my best friend

God made sisters so we could always have a friend

Give a girl the right shoes and she can conquer the world

Thanks for being there when everyone else walked out

Friends are the rainbow in the morning
dewdrop and the fragrance in the evening breeze
Lemonade on a hot summer day
tea in the afternoon or hot chocolate
on a wintry night;
some things just go better with a friend

There once was a little girl with a little curl,
Right in the middle of her forehead.
When she was good she was very good,
but when she was bad, she was horrid! -Longfellow

It's wonderful to have a friend
One on whom you can depend
To chat and giggle with schoolgirl glee,
To sit and sip a cup of tea -LaTourelle

Everyone everywhere
The whole world through
Needs a girlfriend
Just like you!
Others are important
You know we love them, too
Yet, there are special times
When only a girlfriend will do!

Graduation

Congratulations Graduate
You served your time
And learned quite well
Now finally the day is here
When all that love you oh so dear
Can raise their hands and bid you cheer!!

Enjoy this day and all it means
For your journey now begins
So throw your cap into the air
And be proud of how far you've come
Happy Graduation Day!

God is Love

God made the mountains majesty
And oceans bold and restless
He lifted up His hands with light
And painted landscapes breathless
But in a whisper soft and low
He gave to us a child aglow
To come and live with us today
Forever thankful we shall pray
His love for us is ever grand
And so we praise Him as we stand
For giving us His endless grace
To honor holy that precious face
Thank you Lord for all you do
But most of all for Love so true
-Linda LaTourelle

His love can move the mountains
His love can calm the sea
His love is always reaching out
To encircle you and me!
-Thena Smith

◉ Grand-Pa–My Hero

◉ Bounce me one more time, please

◉ Grandmas are just antique little girls

◉ One old crow and a cute little chick live here

◉ My heart belongs to GRANDPA (Grandma)

◉ Nannie's Nest is Best but Papa Rules the Roost

◉ There's no place like home 'ceptin Grandma's

◉ Granny and Papa, love you all the world

◉ Grandpa is my best friend (Grandma)

◉ Nobody does it better, only my Grandma

WALKING WITH GRANDPA
(or Grandma)
I like to walk with Grandpa,
His steps are short like mine.
He doesn't say "Now Hurry Up",
He always takes his time.
I like to walk with Grandpa,
His eyes see thing like mine do -
Wee pebbles bright, a funny cloud,
Half hidden drops of dew.
Most people have to hurry,
They don't stop and see.
I'm glad that God made Grandpa,
Unrushed, and young like me.
-Thena Smith

When I say my prayers at night
I thank the Lord for love so right
My Grandma fills my life with fun
In all the world she's the only one

Grandma, it's important you know
How special you are to me
There is no one quite as precious
Thank you for loving me so
Grandpa,
Can you guess
what I want to be
when I grow up?
As fun and smart as you
Happy Grandfathers' Day

You're–Great, Wise and so Fun
I guess that's why you're called "Grand"pa

It's so great
to have a Grandpa
who loves to play
and have fun,
but the reason
that I love you
is just because
you're the one!
Happy Grandfather's Day Grandpa

Halloween

Carving out memories, one pumpkin at a time -
LaTourelle
Costumes and Pumpkins and Candy Corn, Oh My!
-LaTourelle

Our pumpkin smiles at us
Upon the window sill
We're stuffed with lots of candy
And now feel very ill
-LaTourelle

Hanukkah

Happy Hanukkah to you
Sending you Hanukkah prayers
Hold onto tradition–Happy Hanukkah
As you light each candle, may your heart feel love

Let's light the menorah
For the Festival of Lights,
One candle every evening
For eight great, joyous nights

Humor

◎ On the other hand, we have different fingers.

◎ I hope life isn't a big joke, because I don't get it.

◎ If you go flying back through time and you see somebody else flying forward into the future, it's probably best to avoid eye contact

◎ If you're a cowboy and you're dragging a guy behind your horse, I bet it would really make you mad if you looked back and the guy was reading a magazine

◎ Before you criticize someone, walk a mile in their shoes. That way, you'll be a mile from them, and you'll have their shoes.

◎ A man's got to do what a man's got to do. A woman must do what he can't.

◎ Every time I close the door on reality it comes in through the windows.

◎ I try to take one day at a time, but sometimes several days attack me at once.

◎ Behind every successful woman is a sink full of dishes, basket of laundry and freezer full of fast food.

◎ I bought some powdered water, but I don't know what to add to it -Steven Wright

◎ I saw this guy riding his bike. He was sweating heavily and his hair was blowing through the air. He was going about 50 miles! I started wondering what those straps were strapped around his bike, then I wondered why he was on top of a car. I guess that could explain how fast he was going   -Lara LaTourelle

◎ As the light changed from red to green to yellow and back to red again, I sat there thinking about life. Is that what life is nothing more than a bunch of honking and yelling? Sometimes it seemed that way.

Kwanzaa

May you feel the peace this season
Warmest wishes for happy holidays
Sending you love this Kwanzaa
As you light the candles–Celebrate

Kids Wisdom

Love is foolish, but I still might try it sometime - Keyon, age 12

Love is like an avalanche where you have to run for your life -Pam, age 15

Love is great, especially the candy and flowers on Valentines -Cheryl, age 10

How Do I Love Thee When You're Always Picking Your Nose? -Austin, age 14

I'm not rushing into being in love I'm finding fourth grade hard enough -Lisa, age 9

Love is the most important thing in the world, but basketball is pretty good too -Stephen, age 8

◎ I Am in Love with You Most of the Time, but Don't Bother Me When I'm with My Friends - Jon, age 13

◎ I'm in favor of love as long as it doesn't happen when my favorite show is on television -Randy, age 11

Kindness

◎ A kind word is like a Spring day -Russian Proverb

◎ How beautiful a day can be when kindness touches it! -George Elliston

◎ A bit of fragrance always clings to the hand that gives roses -Chinese Proverb

◎ A man never stands as tall as when he kneels to help a child -Knights of Pythagoras

◎ Sometimes someone says something really small, and it just fits right into this empty place in your heart

◎ Out of all the treasures in the world there is nothing more precious than giving someone a piece of your heart

◎ The best portion of a good man's life is his little nameless, unremembered acts of kindness and of love -William Wordsworth

◎ Those who bring sunshine to the lives of others cannot keep it from themselves. Your kindness has warmed my heart so.

◎ I expect to pass through this world but once. Any good therefore that I can do, or any kindness or abilities that I can show to any fellow creature, let me do it now. Let me not defer it or neglect it, for I shall not pass this way again. -William Penn

◎ Kindness in words creates confidence. Kindness in thinking creates profoundness Kindness in giving creates love -Lao-Tzu

- ⊚ Guard well within yourself that treasure, kindness

- ⊚ Know how to give without hesitation, how to lose without regret, how to acquire without meanness. - George Sand

> Have you had a kindness shown?
> Pass it on;
> 'Twas not given for thee alone,
> Pass it on;
> Let it travel down the years,
> Let it wipe another's tears,
> 'Til in Heaven the deed appears -
> Pass it on.
> -Henry Burton

Love

- ⊚ What a grand thing, to be loved! What a grander thing still, to love! -Victor Hugo
- ⊚ By these words may you always know that my love is with you wherever you go
- ⊚ Dance with me darling, ever so slow. Hold my love in your heart and never let go -LaTourelle
- ⊚ Love is what's left in a relationship after all the selfishness has been removed -Cullen Hightower

How I have loved thee? With all that I am
Joy fills my heart since this love began
Would that I could give you all that I am,
Love lives within me yet more and again -LaTourelle

How do I Love thee?
Let me count the ways–
Hmm, I start with one, right?
-CC Milam

127

Touch my life with tenderness
And fill my cup with love.
Share my dreams as I share
Yours beyond the stars above.

As deep as the ocean
As huge as the sky
You are the
Apple of my eye
-CC Milam

No matter what
No matter where
You take me with
You everywhere-
-August Jones

The most precious possession
that ever comes to a man in
this world is a woman's heart.

Love is honest. Love is true.
Love is what carries us through.
-August Jones

Thanks for memories and blessings you give me throughout my days. For standing close beside me in such immeasurable ways. You are my knight in shining armor and I your maid sweet and fair. Your devotion is to me a love beyond compare.

'Tis you that doth my heart belong
And you I love 'til day is done
How blessed is my love for thee
That I may ever sing joyfully -LaTourelle

The way that you love me is such music divine
Like that old favorite song one hears in their mind
Singing sweet, singing soft, over and over again
With a rhapsody that rings to the depths of my soul
For my love you are the orchestra of life so full
Play me slow, play me gentle, never let go -LaTourelle

■■■■■■■■■■■■■■■■■■■■■■■■■■■■■■

Let us dance with joy so sweet
For in the twinkling of our feet
our spirit and our soul doth meet
-LaTourelle

'Tis you that doth my heart belong
And you I love 'til day is done
How blessed is my love for thee
That I may ever sing joyfully
-LaTourelle

The way that you love me is such music divine
Like that old favorite song one hears in their mind
Singing sweet, singing soft, over and over again
With a rhapsody that rings to the depths of my soul
For my love you are the orchestra of life so full
Play me slow, play me gentle, never let go
-LaTourelle

White puffy clouds that go sailing by
I see as I look up in the baby blue sky
Remind me of special days gone by
Memories of the past come pouring in
My thoughts flow to you once again
And reveal to me how our love did begin.
-CC Milam

Tweedle dee and tweedle dum
Love to play with hugs and fun
Laughter and smiles the whole day through
Oh what a joy when shared by two

Do I love you? Do I love you?
Does the sun still shine?
Do the stars still twinkle?

You are the answer—Love is the question

Say that you love me
Say that it's true
Know that it matters
because I love you

I Love You
I Love You
I Love You
Can you hear me now?

You are-
The sparkle in my eye
Better than strawberry pie
Mittens when it's cold
A treasure worth more than gold
The rhapsody in spring
More precious than anything
Laughter in the sun
Dreams when day is done
All this and so much more
Is everything that I adore

There are no words that tell
The love I have for you
The depths of my feelings
Extend beyond imagination

I want to hold thee in this warmth forever
to feel thy breath encompass me
The rhythm of thy heart doth revive my very soul
Passion ignites fervently within my being,
as thee entwineth thy body around mine
The intimate grasp from thy touch
Has captured all that I am
-LaTourelle

■■■■■■■■■■■■■■■■■■■■■■■■■■■■■■

Love is honest. Love is true.
Love is what carries us through.
-August Jones

Today I found love–Today I found you!

Who am I without you–
Sugar without sweet
Sails without wind
Sand with no sea
Simply put
Love alone

You are to me the rainbow through the rain
You bring the calm before the storm
You are to me the laughter through the pain
You fill my life with everything warm

Memorial Day
Day is done
Gone the sun
From the lake
From the hills
From the sky
All is well
Safely rest
God is nigh
Fading light
dims the sight
And a star
Gems the sky
Gleaming bright
From afar
Drawing nigh
Falls the night
-Major General Daniel Butterfield

Greater love has no one than this, than to lay down his life for his friends
-John 15:13

131

■■■■■■■■■■■■■■■■■■■■■■■■

Missing you–
is missing love
Missing life
Missing breathing
Missing everything
I hate missing

My heart is delicate, so be gentle

Mother's Day

A mother can sing the song of her child's heart, when
they have long since forgotten
Angels are mommies with wings

Best friends forever mom and me
picking flowers and climbing trees.
a shoulder to cry on secrets to share
Warm hearts and hands that really care.

I said a prayer on Mother's Day
to thank the Lord above
for giving me a lifetime full
of your caring and you love.

I thank God for the sacrifice
you've made throughout the years,
for your tenderness and mercy
and chasing away my fears

Youth fades; love droops,
the leaves of friendship fall;
A mother's secret hope outlives them all
-Oliver Wendell Holmes

Mother, you filled my days with fairytales
and my nights with sugar plum dreams
You held my hand for a while,
But my heart is yours forever

Happy is the son whose faith in his mother remains un-challenged -Louisa May Alcott

Her children arise up, and call her blessed -Proverbs 31:28

I remember my mother's prayers and they have always followed me They have clung to me all my life -Lincoln

Motherhood: All love begins and ends there -Browning

My mother had a great deal of trouble with me but I think she enjoyed it -Mark Twain

O ye loving mothers, know ye that in God's sight the best of all ways to worship Him is to educate the children and train them in all the perfections of hu-mankind; and no nobler deed than this can be imagined

New Home

◉ May you find new blessings and joy in your new home

◉ Home is where your heart is. May yours ever be full with love

◉ Happy Housewarming!

◉ Wow–A new beginning!

◉ Bless your home with lots of Love, may angels guide you from above

◉ He is happiest, be he king or peasant, who finds peace in his home -Johann von Goethe

◉ Happy in heart and home is the family that prays to-gether

◉ Bless your new home, may it be a place of beautiful memories for years to come

◉ Home Sweet Home for you, me and baby makes three

◎ Your home is your castle, may you feel like royalty and know that you are rich in love.

◎ God Bless this home so full of love

◎ Fill it with joy and sweetness within every wall

◎ May it be a blessing to all who visit

New Year

The New Year lies before you
Like a spotless tract of snow
Be careful how you tread on it
For every mark will show.

Another year is dawning!
Dear Master, let it be,
on earth, or else in heaven,
Another year for Thee!

Top 10 Most Common New Year Resolutions
1) Lose weight
2) Stop smoking
3) Stick to a budget
4) Save more money
5) Find a better job
6) Become more organized
7) Exercise more
8) Be more patient at work/with others
9) Eat better
10) Become a better person

Should acquaintance be forgot,
And never brought to min'?
Should auld acquaintance be forgot,
And days o' lang syne?
For auld lang syne, my dear,
For auld lang syne,
We'll take a cup o' kindness yet
For auld lang syne -Robert Burns

■ ■

Praise Cards

A Big Hug
A Big Kiss
Awesome
Bravo
Dynamic
Excellent
Exceptional
Fantastic
Good For You
Good Job
Great
Great Discovery
Hip, Hip, Hurray
Hot Dog
How Nice
How Smart
Hurray For You
I Knew You Could Do It
I like You
I Love You!
I Respect You
I Trust You
I'm Proud Of You
Looking Good
Magnificent
Marvelous
Neat
Nice Work
Nothing Can Stop You Now
Outstanding Performance
Spectacular
Super Job

Try a word of praise to anyone you love. Watch them give you more than they ever did before. Everyone is needing to know that they matter. So write a little note and share a special word. Try one or more of these and bless someone.

■ ■

Prayers

Sometimes God calms the storms and sometimes He lets
the storm rage and calms His child. May you feel the
wave of His love embracing you with peace

THE WONDER OF IT ALL

I stand in awe before you, Lord
As I watch my child at play.
How precious is each action
and each word I hear him say.
I know that as You look down on us
We are so very small.
Yet, You know each tiny grain of sand
and by name you know us all!
Lord, though my child seems small to me
as he stands upon your shore,
I know that were he ten feel tall-
You could not love him more.
I cannot even fathom Lord,
How great your love must be
but I know that it is greater still
than the vastness of your sea.
I stand in humble reverence Lord
As I watch my child in play
and know that you watch over me
in much the self same way!
And so I say a prayer of thanks
Dear Lord of earth and sea
for all the loving care you give
to both my child and me.
-Thena Smith

■■■■■■■■■■■■■■■■■■■■■■■■■■■■

Retirement

Yesterday I was working so hard
And at the end of the day
I was exhausted and TIRED.
But today the sun can rise and set
And I can remember
Or I can forget.
I can get up if I've had enough sleep
Or go back to bed
And count some more sheep.
I can get dressed and go out
Or stay in my jammies all day
Clean my house or go out and play.
I can dine on peanut butter and jelly
Or toast and muffins
Or I can buy lunch and cook nuthin'.
Oh, how wonderful just adding a "RE"
In front of "Tired"
Can make your world be!!
-Thena Smith

Happy Retirement

Now you can catch up on those naps.
Think of the long lunch breaks
Time for some R & R

Now as you retire
Take the time to be with family
Have fun, keep active
Make new friends
Kick your heels up
Throw out the clock

■■■■■■■■■■■■■■■■■■■■■■■■■■

Romance

Are flowers the winter's choice?
Is love's bed always snow?
She seemed to hear my silent voice,
Not love's appeals to know
I never saw so sweet a face
As that I stood before
My heart has left its dwelling-place
And can return no more

Doubt that the stars are fire; doubt that
The sun doth move; doubt truth to be a
Liar, but never doubt that I love -Shakespeare

I gently touched her hand; she gave
A look that did my soul enslave;
I pressed her rebel lips in vain:
They rose up to be pressed again
Thus happy, I no farther meant,
Than to be pleased and innocent

Give me a kiss, add to that kiss a score;
Then to that twenty, add a hundred more:
A thousand to that hundred: so kiss on,
To make that thousand up a million
Treble that million, and when that is done,
Let's kiss afresh, as when we first begun
-Robert Herrick

◎ Some Enchanted Evening

◎ Your kisses set my heart on fire

◎ To the rose of my heart–I Love You

◎ I am your canvas–Paint me with your love

- When I listen to my heart...it whispers your name

- I only thought about you once today-I just never stopped

- Thou art to me a delicious torment-Ralph Waldo Emerson

- I believe in long, slow, deep, soft, wet kisses that last three days

- The softest thing in the world will overcome the hardest Lao-tsu

- Won't you come into my garden? I would like my roses to see you!

- For as many times as the waves caress the shore, that's how much I love you

- Whenever I think of perfect things, you're the first one that comes to my mind.

- In order to be irreplaceable one must always be different -Coco Channel

- The very first moment I beheld him, my heart was irrevocably gone -Jane Austen

- Come live with me, and be my love and we will all the pleasures prove -Christopher Marlowe

- Love distills desire upon the eyes, love brings bewitching grace into the heart-Euripides-

- My love is like a tattered rose pressed into the pages of time. Each time a page is turned the memories flood back in reminding me of a love so grand when once I was so young.

◉ I believe in the sun even when it is not shining; in love even when I am alone, and in God even when he is silent

◉ Other men it is said have seen angels, but I have seen thee and thou art enough. -George Moore

◉ Anyone can be passionate, but it takes real lovers to be silly. Thanks for being outrageously hysterical!

◉ I sought him whom my soul lovest, I found him, I held him and I would not let him go -Song of Solomon

◉ Sensual pleasure passes in the twinkling of an eye, but the friendship between us, the mutual confidence, the delights of the heart, the enchantment of the soul, these things do not perish and can never be destroyed I shall love you until I die -Voltaire

◉ Can I have your picture so I can show Santa what I want for Christmas?

Seasons

◉ In The Good Ol' Summertime

◉ Love is the light of Christmas

◉ Even when it's cold outside our memories will keep us warm. Want to snuggle

◉ Snowflakes Are Angel Kisses. Pucker up!

◉ Spring's greatest joy beyond a doubt is when it brings the children out -Edgar Guest

◉ A Crisp Winter's Breeze

◉ A Rainbow of colors all on the ground

- 'Tis sweet perfume of lilacs scenting the morning breeze
  As melodious robin redbreast awakens me with his call
  The roses wind with laziness and such a gentle ease
  Oh what a wonderful blessing, the wonder of it all
  -LaTourelle

- Winter snow in the warmth of a fire fills my heart with love's desire

- In the heat of a summer's eve I fell in love with you

- Softly has a new snow you crept into my life

- Kissed by the breath of spring your heart pounding into my soul, we embrace the innocence of our youth and come together in passionate closeness as our hearts become of one accord in love

- The vineyards are blazing with the blush of fall, this harvest has been the most blessed of all -LaTourelle

- Winter is an etching, spring a watercolor, summer an oil painting and autumn a mosaic of them all - Horowitz

- Laughter is the sun that drives winter from the human face

- The future lies before you like a path of driven snow. Be careful how you tread on it for every mark will show

The Year's at the spring
And the day's at the morn;
Morning's at seven;
The hillside's dew-pearled;
The lark's on the wing;
The snail's on the thorn:
God's in his heaven--
All's right with the world!
~By Robert Browning

Thought is the blossom;
language the bud;
action the fruit behind it
~Ralph Waldo Emerson

to be refreshed by a morning walk
or an evening saunter.
to be thrilled by the stars at night;
to be elated over a bird's nest or
a wildflower in spring
these are some of the rewards
of the simple life
~John Burroughs

St. Patrick's Day

- The Luck of the Irish–Happy St Patty's Day
- Feelin' Green
- Leapin' Leprechauns
- Top o' the morning
- God and his angels close at hand,
  Friends and family, their love impart,
  And Irish blessings in your heart!
- May your right hand always be stretched out in
  friendship and never in want

I'm looking over a four leaf clover
That I over-looked before.
One leaf is sunshine, the second is rain,
Third is the roses that grows in the lane.
No need explaining the one remaining
Is somebody I adore.

Secret Pal

Thinking of You
You are in my thoughts today
and just a prayer away!
Your Secret Pal
-CC Milam

Love is kind
Love is true
Love is the friendship
between me and you
Your Secret Pal
-CC Milam

Dear Secret Pal,
It is hard to believe the time
is here for you to know.
As I think through the year,
where did the time go?
 I have enjoyed each month
and the thoughts of you
praying the Lord would bless
in everything that you do
 May He continue to lead you and guide
and always keep you close by His side.
In His Love,
Your Secret Pal
-CC Milam

Spiritual

- ☺ No matter what is happening in your life, know that God is waiting for you with open arms

- ☺ Do your best and then sleep in peace God is awake

- ☺ God has a purpose for me no one else can fulfill

- Begin to weave and God will give you the thread
- Sometimes when God says "no", it's because He has something better in store for you
- Prayer: don't bother to give God instructions, just report for duty
- It's my business to do God's business and it's His business to take care of my business
- How come you're always running around looking for God? He's not lost
- God put me on earth to accomplish a number of things; right now I'm so far behind I will live forever!
- You will seek Me and find Me when you seek Me with all your heart
- Nothing shines so brightly as the gleam in a child's eyes -Sherry Moss
- Stop and think of all you have and you will know God is responsible for it all -Sherry Moss
- When I gaze upon the fields of green I see the wonders of God's love -Sherry Moss
- When I look to the sky so blue and white I see the miracle of His promise -Sherry Moss
- When I lay my head down on my pillow at night I know I am blessed with God's love, by my side -Sherry Moss

Stress

- I'm a little stressed right now—just turn around and leave quietly and no one gets hurt. -Weaver
- To avoid stress at home—wear pearls and high heels—June Cleaver always looked great!

I'm feeling rather sassy today
Nothing can frighten me!
Nothing is going to cause me stress
I'm as strong as I can be!!

No one is going to get me down
Or cause me to whimper and whine
You have to treat me with respect
I've earned it, it is mine!

I'm going to tackle all those tasks
That seem to overwhelm
There's a new woman steering this ship-
A toughie at the helm.

I'm—oh what is that awful sound?
That ringing in my ear?
Oh, it's my alarm clock going off
Time to wake up, I fear!!!
-Thena Smith

Lord God in Heaven above
I know you bless the ones you love
And I hope that when you bless
You overlook this awful mess!

The kids are fussy
And the hubby is grumpy
The beds aren't made
And the gravy is lumpy.

But my home is full
Of the ones I love best
So I ask you Lord
To bless this mess!

Sympathy

For some moments in life there are no words -Willy
Wonka

I am here to lift you up
To brighten all your days
My arms will gladly hold you
And wipe your tears away
-LaTourelle

I have no words to express my sorrow, but only my
love and the tears I will shed tomorrow.

Family is precious and dear to me and to lose one
breaks my heart you see. I know he is in a better
place, for he is seeing Jesus face to face. So where
do we go from here you might say,I think we
should first pray. And read our Bibles to see what
He has told. And to live life like Jesus has showed.
-August Jones for his Uncle Chester Jones

Let me be your hope when life seems desperate
Let me be your laughter crying through the tears
Let me be the touch that will lift your spirits
Let me be the heart beating strong for you
Let me be your strength when you're feeling weak
Let me be everything to you
-LaTourelle

Even if I'm hurting today, if I'll look forward to
tomorrow, for there's a very thin line between happiness and sorrow

In those moments of sorrow, look up for your Father
is weeping with you. Call to His name and His heart
will comfort you. -LaTourelle

■■■■■■■■■■■■■■■■■■■■■■■■■■■

What though the radiance, which was once so bright, Be now forever taken from my sight, Though nothing can bring back the hour of my splendor in the grass, of glory in the flowers; We will grieve not, rather find strength in what remains behind -Wordsworth

I didn't invent the rainy day, I just carry the best umbrella. Let me help with the storm.

I will shield you from the storm says the Lord and calm the wildest sea. Reach out your heart and follow me.

One must learn to be still in the midst of turmoil to feel the unmistakable presence of strength Loneliness is the prison of the human spirit□please let my love set you free

'Hope' is the thing with feathers -- That perches in the soul and sings the tune without the words and never stops–at all. -Emily Dickinson

When you look to the sky, know this: there are more stars shining inside of you than in all of the heavens above -Lydia Carfield

Love is what will carry you through these difficult times Please know there are those here who will hold you up for as long as you need Just hold out your hand and know that we are here

In times of sorrow let the spirit of love be your wings to fly you to a sweeter land

Wishing we could be by your side at this time, our deepest sympathy

Wishing you a day of special moments in this time of sorrow and treasured memories to lift you up

Wishing you hope in the midst of sorrow, comfort in the midst of pain

With heartfelt sympathy and kindest thoughts to you in your sorrow

May the concern and sympathy of those who care help you through this difficult time

Don't let your grief be measured by her worth for then your sorrow has no end -Shakespeare

I'll be a friend to see you through the night, arms to hold you ever so tight, a candle always burning bright and love that wants to make everything right -LaTourelle

Lonely? Call - 1-I LOVE YOU

Nestled in God s Arms
The Lord loves little ones
And keeps them safe and warm
In a special place in Heaven
Nestled in His arms.
The lord placed the tiny babes
To grow in a mother s womb
And if He calls them home before their birth
He must have them a special room.
I have not yet seen Heaven
But I know our God above
Will take special care of tiny ones
And surround them with His love.
So do not fret or mourn
For the tiny soul set free
But look forward to a reunion
That will last eternally.
-Thena Smith

Teacher's Day

Thank you for your lasting
impression on my life

You are a very special teacher
Always giving and sharing
Teaching us to love learning
And showing us love by caring

Teachers are so special
To every girl and boy
They fill our minds with knowledge
And making learning such a joy

Thanks for teaching me to love learning and others

Some people come into our lives and quickly go
others stay and leave footprints on our hearts
and we are forever changed as a person

You've been more than a teacher to me
You've been a friend
Happy Teacher's Day

Education is not the filling of a bucket but the
lighting of a fire. -W.B. Yeats

Thanks for being such a wonderful teacher to my
child and making a difference to him/her

A teacher affects eternity; he can never tell
where his influence stops. -Henry Adams

To learn and never be filled is wisdom
To teach and never be weary is love

In the service of the Lord, it is not
where you serve, but how -J. Reuben Clark, Jr.

Thanks

I will give thanks to Thee, for I am fearfully and wonderfully made -Book of Psalms

You've done so many nice things for me I don't know where to start—Eeny meeney—thanks!

How does one thank you
For all the things you do?
I do not know what we would have done
Had it not been for you!

How do we express our feelings
For the things you did for us
Never expecting gratitude or praise
And never wanting a fuss?

All I can do is say "Thank You"
And hope that the meaning is clear
That is a deep heart felt thanks
And pray that it's depth your heart can hear!
-Thena Smith

How does one thank you
For all the things you do?
In the dictionary under generosity
Should be a photo of you!

Blessed are those that can give without remembering
and receive without forgetting

No duty is more urgent than that of returning thanks.
From the bottom of my heart you have touched my
life. Thank you so much for everything.

Let us be grateful to people who make us happy;
they are the charming gardeners who make our
souls blossom -Marcel Proust

■ ■

G ratitude is the heart's memory
In our daily workaday world
Sometimes it's hard to impart
All the love and gratitude
That's in our heart.
Sometimes there seems to be
No words to say
That you enrich our lives
And bless our day.
But with this little book
Let us try to show you
Just how we really feel
As our feelings of friendship
and love we reveal.
This little book can only begin
To thank you for all you do
And most of all to express
Just how grateful we are for you!
-Thena Smith

◉ Contentment is not the fulfillment of what you want,
but the realization of how much you already have

◉ Thank you Lord, for my family. There are
many who are lonely

Thank you for Business
Just a little thanks for your giant blessing
Friends like you are wonderful. Thanks for your
business
It is with great pleasure we welcome you
Just wanted to say Thank You for your business
With special thanks and much appreciation
For your friendship, your business and the opportu-
nity to serve you, thank you

Thanksgiving

For each new morning with its light,
For rest and shelter of the night,
For health and food, for love and friends,
For everything Thy goodness sends.
-Ralph Waldo Emerson

Do not get tired of doing what is good. Don't get discouraged and give up, for we will reap a harvest of blessing at the appropriate time -Book of Galatians

The Turkey is a funny bird
His head goes wobble wobble,
but all that he can ever say,
is Gobble, Gobble, Gobble.

Happy Thanksgiving

Ain't nothing like Mama's holiday cookin'
to make a body warm

Mama's in the kitchen, cookin' up a storm,
Daddy's on the sofa keepin' it warm

Pumpkin pie and cranberry bread
color the table with love

The vineyards are blazing with the blush of fall,
this harvest has been the most blessed of all

Forever on Thanksgiving Day the heart
will find the pathway home -Roger North

Let us give thanks to the Lord up above, Who bless us each day with His grace and love. Thank you, Lord, for each new day you bring, We lift up our voice and with praises we sing. Glory, honor, and praises to you! For all the blessings you give, we thank you. -Linda LaTourelle

Thinking of You

Our lives are sewn together with threads of loving care. Each day we're blessed with opportunities to share and so I take this moment to send some thoughts your way. Wrapped in love and goodness as I think of you and pray -LaTourelle

This is what I wish for you—
joyous times beyond compare
someone who is always there
comfort when days are blue
hugs to always shelter you
peace like a dove
faith from above
summer sunsets on a winter's night
birds that sing on winged flight
rainbows after every storm
sunny days to keep you warm
kisses from lips so sweet
twinkling toes and dancing feet
all of this and so much more
is sent with love to the one I adore
-LaTourelle

Did you know?

Did you know that I wanted to see you smile?
Did you know I'd walk that extra mile?
Did you know there is only one love so true?
Did you know that person is simply you?
-LaTourelle

153

Did anyone ever tell you how special you are?
Did anyone ever tell you
just how much that they love you?
Did anyone ever tell you
how important you make others feel?
Well, someone is now and that someone is me!

One hour with thee ! When sun is set,
Oh, what can teach me to forget
The thankless labours of the day;
The hopes, the wishes, flung away;
The increasing wants, and lessening gains,
The master's pride, who scorns my pains?
One hour with thee -Sir Walter Scott

Valentine's Day

◉ Give me what you alone can give,
A kiss to build a dream on

◉ Cupid, draw back your arrow
Straight to my lover's heart for me

◉ I love you for sentimental reasons

◉ True Love

◉ My Heart's Desire

◉ Hugs and Kisses

◉ Will You Be My Valentine?

◉ My Funny Valentine

◉ You Hold The Key to My Heart

◉ Love Letters

◉ Love Bugs

◉ Bee Mine

- Be still my heart and be mine
- SWAK! And a hug, too
- Two-lips just for you
- When A Man Loves A Woman
- Whosoever loves believes the impossible
- You must remember this, a kiss is still a kiss. . .
- You're all I need my love, my valentine
- The sweetest joy, the wildest woe is love
- To love is to believe–to hope–to know
- Two souls with but a single thought.
  Two hearts that beat as one. -Bellinghausen
- If I could wrap love in a ribbon, it would be
  my gift to you
- You are what happened when I wished upon a star
- Candy Kisses and Champagne Wishes
- Won't you be "My Valentine"

These are my gifts for you
Three little words that
Ring so sweet to my ears
Simply put-I Love You

You are as fair and sweet and tender,
Dear brown-eyed little sweetheart mine,
As when, a callow youth and slender,
I asked to be your Valentine.

So take, dear love, this little token,
And if there speaks in any line
The sentiment I'd fain have spoken,
Say, will you kiss your Valentine?

Veteran's Day

IN FLANDERS FIELDS.

In Flanders field the poppies blow
Between the crosses, row on row,
That mark our place; and in the sky
The larks, still bravely singing, fly
Scarce heard amid the guns below.
We are the Dead. Short days ago
We lived, felt dawn, saw sunset glow,
Loved and were loved, and now we lie
In Flanders fields.
Take up our quarrel with the foe:
To you from failing hands we throw
The torch; be yours to hold it high.
If ye break with us who die
We shall not sleep, though poppies grow
In Flanders fields.
-Major John McCrae, May 1915

Wedding

⊚ And the two shall be called One

⊚ Two hearts, Two souls, One love, Forever

⊚ All my love, all my life, Always & Forever

⊚ Because You Loved Me

⊚ Blissfully Wedded

⊚ Can You Feel the Love Tonight?

⊚ Could I Have This Dance

⊚ First love, last love

⊚ For hearing my thoughts, understanding my
dreams and being my best friend, For filling my
life with joy and loving me without end, I do

- Happiness is being married to your best friend.
- Have I Told You Lately that I Love You?
- He Loves Me, He Loves Me Not, He Loves Me
- I Wanna Grow Old With You
- Love is patient; love is kind; love never ends.
- If I know what love is, it is because of you.
- And the two shall become one
- Happiness is marrying your best friend.
- Be one in heart and always in mind
- Love is friendship set to music
- A Match made in heaven
- And the story begins
- Tonight is a celebration of you!
- A kiss to build a dream on
- A Celebration of Love
- To the Bride and Groom
- With all that I am and all that I have and all that I hope to be I will honor you with my life forever
- May the wings of angels carry you forever with this moment of wedded bliss always in your heart
- As I give you my hand to hold, I give you my heart to keep
- From long ago and far away, love brought to our wedding day!
- Congratulations on this your special day
- Best wishes for a long and happy marriage

The road is bright before us,
As hand in had we start,
We'll travel on together,
One mind, one soul, one heart.

From this day forward
How do we express our feelings
For the things you did for us

How do I love thee?
Let me count the ways.
I love thee to the depth
And breadth & height
My soul can reach,
I love thee with the breath,
Smiles, tears of all my life!

When I fall in love,
It will be forever.
When I give my heart,
It will be completely
-Edward Heyman

If ever two were one, then surely we. If ever man were loved by wife, then thee. -Anne Bradstreet

How sweet it is to be loved by you. -Eddie Holland

Where your treasure is, there will your heart be also. -New Testament

Woman was created from the rib of man, not from his head to be above him, nor his feet to be walked upon, But from his side to be equal, near his arm to be protected and close to his heart to be loved.

Wisdom

We are all artists gently guided by our Master's hand, painting a vision called life The blending of colors like joy, sorrow, wisdom and love inspire us to create a magnificent masterpiece of self -Linda LaTourelle

Imagination Is the SOUL within
-LaTourelle

Life is a song--sing it.
Life is a game--play it.
Life is a challenge--meet it.
Life is a dream--realize it.
Life is a sacrifice--offer it.
Life is love--enjoy it.

It is not in the pursuit of happiness that we find fulfillment, it is in the happiness of pursuit
-Denis Waitley

What lies behind us, and what lies before us are tiny matters compared to what lies within us. -Emerson

From the moment of birth until our last breath our life is a unique story unfolding. Tales of faith, hope and trials; of miracles, adventures and romance; of joys, sorrows and love, blend harmoniously together to reveal the wonder of God's purpose in bestowing upon us this incredible gift of life. Yea, we are fearfully and wonderfully made and what we do with this blessing called life is our gift to God. Moment by moment our life's journey is a distinctively unique narrative illuminating our Creator's awesome love for us. -Linda LaTourelle

If you look at what you have in life,
You'll always have more.
If you look at what you don't have
in life, you'll never have enough -Oprah Winfrey

When we do the best that we can, we never know
what miracle is wrought in our life, or in the life of
another -Helen Keller

The person who tries to live alone will not succeed
as a human being. His heart withers if it does not
answer another heart. His mind shrinks away if he
hears only the echoes of his own thoughts and finds
no other inspiration

The purpose of life is a life of purpose

The happiest moments of my life have been the few
which I have passed at home in the bosom of my
family -Thomas Jefferson

Your life is made up of years that mean nothing;
moments that mean all.

Always do right. This will amaze most people, and
astonish the rest. -Mark Twain

Deal with the faults of others as gently as your own

Every good thought you think is contributing its
share to the ultimate result of your life

Doing the best at this moment puts you in the best
place for the next moment

Oh, the places you'll go, oh, the things you'll see

- ◎ If you live in the present, every moment is a new beginning
- ◎ Heal the past, live the present, dream the future -Mary Engelbreit
- ◎ Think highly of yourself because the world takes you at your own estimate
- ◎ I am more than I know myself to be
- ◎ Someone's opinion of you does not have to become your reality."-- Les Brown

Sometimes you just have to hold your head up high, and blink away the tears

Ask God for guidance and then hang on for the Ride!

-Rose Kennedy

Woman to Woman

What came first, the woman or the department store? Let's go shopping

I'm still hot, it just comes in flashes

Love is blind—marriage is a real eye-opener

If he asks what kind of books you like tell him checkbooks are your preference

Remember my name, you'll be screaming it later

Of course I don't look busy—I did it right the first time

The female's rules are subject to change at a moment's notice—no questions asked

I don't believe in miracles...I rely on them

And your point is...

Dear Friend,

This is a subject that has been dear to my heart for years and years. It seems apparent with the way the world is now that too often we neglect the people we love most. We get caught up in day to day living and unfortunately forget that our family needs to hear and see our love. One way you can do this is through writing. Don't think that you can't write, because you know how to talk, thus you can write. Tell them your feelings. All you really need to do is put on to paper what you feel in your heart–simple and sweet!

My prayer is that you will make some time soon and sit down to put your love on paper in the form of a journal or a love letter to each member of your family. I have even done circle journaling with my girls, at times, to share our feelings with each other. People don't care how you say it, they just care that you do.

If you have children or a parent, take the time now, while you have the time, no matter how young or old your family is and write to them, for them and for you. I promise you that it will be one of the most precious blessings you can give to them. Husband, wife, son, daughter, parent, sister or brother–your gift will be a treasure to them and future generations.

Blessings,
Linda

■■■■■■■■■■■■■■■■■■■■■■■■■■■■■■

In the twilight of your childhood
may the memories linger long
to be carefree and innocent
is what will keep you young
don't worry over silly stuff
that doesn't mean that much
just focus on the blessings
that are right within your touch
because my darling daughters
time will fly so swiftly past
you'll wonder where it all went
and how you grew up so fast
your grandma used to tell me
when I was young like you
that all the dreams I hope for
sometimes do come true
remember this my sweethearts
that mother loves you too
I pray for your success in life
knowing God will see you through
my fervent prayer for you this year
is that you will seek His face
for no matter where life leads you
may it be by his guiding grace
you have always been the best in me
I've been blessed beyond compare
God gave to me the gift of you
and a love that is so rare
so on this Christmas morning
will you take this gift of love
a treasure I bestow on you
sent to me from our father above.
-Linda LaTourelle
December 21, 2003

This poem was written for my beautiful Daughters as a gift on Christmas 2003

~

I Love You Girls With all my Heart ~ You're the Best!

-Momma

When first I heard your cry
my heart wept joyfully so,
for in that wee small voice
came a love that I would
know. You are a precious angel
sent to change my life
to teach me about giving
and most of all sacrifice.
From that day forward
you had my heart
with a love so special
none can tear apart.
-Linda LaTourelle

Dear Daughters,

Seems like only yesterday that you were born, the memory of that moment will forever linger on. You came to me with divine guidance and have captured my heart for evermore. Your beauty is beyond compare and the young women you are becoming is such an incredible joy to watch. I remember you as babies and wondered what you'd look like at every stage. God has been so good to us and I am so blessed to call you my daughters. I want you to know, I love you with every part of my being from the beginning, and now through eternity. Thank you for the joy you give so lovingly to me everyday of my life. You are precious in His sight and mine. May your life be as blessed as mine has.

Forever and Always
-Momma

■■■■■■■■■■■■■■■■■■■■■■■■■■

The sun threw itself upon your skin
The cross slit thy skin
And you seemed heavily thin
They drove thorns into your head
And blood was shed
Not for loyalty
Not for honor
But for your father
They set you up against that cross
And your back was aching
They pounded the hammer in your hands
And your eyes were of sorrow
They pounded each nail into each foot
But love was all you had to give
Everyone stood in shock and shame
Very few were in sorrow
All you had was love to give
And wanted us not to refuse
Many don't understand
Many won't
But many share your message

Written by Lara, a 14 year old homeschooled girl
who has a love for writing and has been very inspired by the wonderful J.R.R. Tolkien trilogy,
The Lord of the Rings. She is in the process of
writing a book in the style of Tolkien, because of
her love for his writing and her love for reading.

I love to hear the 'remember when's',
The times we had with all our friends,
But there's one person that means the most,
The one I'd give a well-deserved toast....
She's been by my side,
And stayed in my heart,
Our friendship is strong,
And will never part.
BEST FRIENDS FOREVER

There are times that we must ask ourselves
how much do I love this person
and my answer—
words could not explain just how much

You cook–thank you. You clean–thank you
you ignore the fact that I sit on the couch
and do nothing all day–thank you
I LOVE YOU!

Have you heard? Have you heard the big news?
You're the best friend I've ever had!

Our friendship is like a song
with the perfect melody!
Thanks for always being there!

You know, eventually you stop believing in things
like Santa, the Tooth Fairy, and the Easter Bunny
but I'll never stop believing in you
You're the best friend a girl could have!

Nicole–What can I say! She is a sweetheart and so fun.
A delightful friend of my daughters and someone that
I have enjoyed getting to know. She lovingly helped
to add some great verses to this new book of mine. I
thank you, Nicole. May it bless you in a special way!
Thanks for you help and the fun chats!

■■■■■■■■■■■■■■■■■■■■■■■■■■■■■■

ABBREVIATIONS

Alabama	AL	Oklahoma	OK
Alaska	AK	Oregon	OR
American Samoa	AS	Palau	PW
Arizona	AZ	Pennsylvania	PA
Arkansas	AR	Puerto Rico	PR
California	CA	Rhode Island	RI
Colorado	CO	South Carolina	SC
Connecticut	CT	South Dakota	SD
Delaware	DE	Tennessee	TN
District of Columbia	DC	Texas	TX
Fed States of Micronesia	FM	Utah	UT
Florida	FL	Vermont	VT
Georgia	GA	Virgin Island	VI
Hawaii	HI	Virginia	VA
Idaho	ID	Washington	WA
Illinois	IL	West Virginia	WV
Indiana	IN	Wisconsin	WI
Iowa	IA	Wyoming	WY
Kansas	KS		
Kentucky	KY	***Canadian Abbreviations***	
Louisiana	LA	Alberta	AB
Maine	ME	British Columbia	BC
Marshall Islands	MH	Manitoba	MB
Maryland	MD	New Brunswick	NB
Massachusetts	MA	Newfoundland -Labrador	NL
Michigan	MI	Northwest Territories	NT
Minnesota	MN	Nova Scotia	NS
Mississippi	MS	Ontario	ON
Missouri	MO	Prince Edward Island	PE
Montana	MT	Quebec	QC
Nebraska	NE	Saskatchewan	SK
Nevada	NV	Yukon	YT
New Hampshire	NH	American Samoa	AS
New Jersey	NJ	Guam	GU
New Mexico	NM	Marshall Islands	MH
New York	NY	Northern Mariana Islands	MP
North Carolina	NC	Palau	PW
North Dakota	ND	Puerto Rico	PR
Ohio	OH	Virgin Islands	VI

■■■■■■■■■■■■■■■■■■■■■■■■■■■■■■■

HOLIDAYS & CELEBRATIONS

January
New Year's Eve
New Year's Day
Martin Luther King Jr. Day
Twelfth Night
Epiphany
Jewish New Year of the Trees
Chinese New Year
Australia Day

February
Groundhog Day
Black History Month
Mardi Gras
President's Day
Valentine's Day
Leap Year

March
Lent
Ash Wednesday
International Women's Day
St. Patrick's Day
Greek Independence Day

April
April Fool's Day
Passover
Easter
Palm Sunday
Holy Thursday
Good Friday
Easter Sunday
Arbor Day
Earth Day
St. George's Day

May
May Day
Cinco de Mayo
Memorial Day
Mother's Day
Citizenship Day - Canada
Victoria Day

June
Father's Day

Flag Day
Summer Solstice

July
Canada Day
Fourth of July

August
Hiroshima Day

September
Labor Day
National Grandparents Day
See you at the Pole
Autumn Equinox
International Day of Peace
Jewish High Holy Days
Rosh Hashanah
Yom Kippur

October
Octoberfest
Canadian Thanksgiving
Columbus Day
Halloween

November
Guy Fawkes Day
Remembrance Day
Veteran's Day
US Thanksgiving
St. Catherine's Day
Ramadan
St. Andrew's Day

December
Advent
Chanukah
St. Nicholas Day
St. Lucia Day
Winter Solstice
Christmas Eve
Christmas Day
Boxing Day
St. Stephen's Day
Kwanzaa
Twelve Days of Christmas
Holy Innocents

■■■■■■■■■■■■■■■■■■■■■■■■■

BIRTHSTONES & FLOWERS

January
Garnet ~ Constancy
Carnation
February
Amethyst ~ Sincerity
Violet
March
Aquamarine ~ Courage
Daffodil
April
Diamond ~ Innocence
Sweet Pea, Daisy
May
Emerald ~ Success
Lily of the Valley
June
Pearl ~ Health
Rose
July
Ruby ~ Contentment
Larkspur
August
Peridot ~ Happiness
Poppy
September
Sapphire ~ Clear Thinking
Morning Glory
October
Opal ~ Hope
Calendula
November
Topaz ~ Fidelity
Chrysanthemum
December
Turquoise ~ Prosperity
Holly

■■■■■■■■■■■■■■■■■■■■■■■■■■■■■■

ANNIVERSARY GIFTS
Traditional and Modern

1st	Paper	Clocks
2nd	Cotton	China
3rd	Leather	Crystal, Glass
4th	Linen, Silk	Electrical Appliances
5th	Wood	Silverware
6th	Iron	Wood
7th	Wool, Copper	Desk Sets
8th	Bronze	Linen, Laces
9th	Pottery, China	Leather
10th	Tin, Aluminum	Diamond Jewelry
11th	Steel	Fashion Jewelry
12th	Silk	Pearls
13th	Lace	Textiles, Furs
14th	Ivory	Gold Jewelry
15th	Crystal	Watches
20th	China	Platinum
25th	Silver	Sterling Silver
30th	Pearl	Diamond
35th	Coral	Jade
40th	Ruby	Ruby
45th	Sapphire	Sapphire
50th	Gold	Gold
55th	Emerald	Emerald
60th	Diamond	Diamond

These are ideas for wedding anniversary gifts that may be of help when selecting a gift or creating a card for someone special.

■ ■

Contributors to this Book

Thena Smith– What a surprise when Linda LaTourelle found my website a few weeks ago and contacted me about using some of my poetry. I was even more amazed to find out that she was from Kentucky, a few miles from where I was born and raised in Lowes, Ky. Isn't it funny that I had to move to California to meet her and she moved from California to Kentucky and ultimately met me. Amazing what a small world exists when God has a plan. Since our first lovely chat via e-mail, we are enjoying a blossoming friendship.

Recently retired, I am delighted to have moved beyond life in the fast lane to a place where I can focus on things that matter like scrapbooking and writing. For as long as I can remember I have written. At age seven, my poem was published. My mother was a fine poet and she was an inspiration and encouragement. Like most women then, her busy life left little time for writing. My grandmother tutored me in "elocution". In those days it was a formal style of teaching the art of eloquent diction that resulted in an impressive writing style.

A few years ago a friend and I co-wrote and produced a children's musical for our local church. Later, we did another collage of poetry and songs, which were televised by our local cable company. Everyone should have a moment that they enjoy as much as I enjoyed those!

I am happily married to Ron, my sweetheart. We just celebrated our anniversary of 38 years. Together we share the love of our beautiful daughter, Melissa, age unmentionable (LOL).

I was happy to share some of my verses with Linda and pleased that she wants to share them with you. My dream has always been to have a book of poetry published in order to share more easily with those who enjoy it. Linda understood and appreciated that dream immediately and working together, with God's help, we plan to make that dream a reality! Keep your eye on www. theultimateword.com for news of this coming creation.

A note from the author: As one of Thena's large following said, "You are scrap royalty to me!" It is with pleasure that I agree, thankful for the friendship we share.. She is truly an inspiration and joy to my life. She has been a tremendous help on this book. We have plans for a "Thena" book, so keep watching! Thanks so much, Thena.

Todd Jones—Originally from Glasgow, Kentucky, Todd lives in east Tennessee with his wife Cindy. Together they homeschool their children Will, Olivia and Garrett (well, really Cindy does, but Dad helps). He expresses his artistic talent through graphic and structural design by day. At night, he moonlights as a wannabe bassist, playing a variety of music. In getting to know Todd, it is easy to sense his love for the Lord. He is an extremely talented man with great vision and insight, with a giving heart, too. A blessing indeed!

Sherry Moss—Contributing from Nicholasville, Kentucky, near Lexington, she has been my mentor and sounding board, as well as contributing a few verses included in this book. Her experience in this industry has been invaluable. I look forward to the opportunity to share all of this at HIA in Dallas this coming February. She is a multi-talented lady. Her love for the Lord is one of many common bonds we share, along with laughter and support, Sherry is a joy to know and a blessing to call her my friend.

August Jones—A husband, a father, a radiographer. August writes in his spare time. He believes all inspiration comes from God. He writes from his heart and as a testimony of God's love and grace. His greatest desire is for everyone to seek God for forgiveness, accept Jesus Christ into their heart and live for Him each and everyday. (No Todd and August are not related. They've never ever talked to each other.)

CC Milam—A follower of the Lord Jesus Christ, a wife, a mother, a homemaker & a teacher. CC has had a passion for poetry and writing since she was very young. Being an only child, she used poetry to express her innermost feelings of sadness and joy. Today, she still expresses herself through writing. She feels that it helps her capture a moment in time that can be remembered through words. She hopes that her writings help others to relate and feel peace, joy and comfort. These can only truly be experienced by knowing Jesus Christ as your personal Lord and Savior. Her prayer is that you will experience His abundant love and overflowing grace.

To each of you, I am so blessed by your love and goodness and am honored to call you friend. I couldn't have done it without you. Thank you so much for your support.

■■■■■■■■■■■■■■■■■■■■■■■■■■■■■

Barbara Cox—My first poem wasn't written until I was in my 40's and came with the birth of my first grandson that was born a mere 1 pound 12 oz. My mother and father my husband and home are gone but, before God called them home he blessed me with a wonderful son, two beautiful daughters and 12 grandchildren... plus, many true and loving friends... My best friend in High School calls me long distance every night to make sure that I am doing ok.. To see my poetry in print has always been a dream for me... and through you that dream has come as a Christmas Present.

RESOURCES
rubberstamps

Dee Gruenig and the entire Posh Impressions team are delighted to be included as a source for Linda LaTourelle's new book.

Posh Impressions remains a creative and contributing force for Rubber Stamping and Scrapbooking, and has since 1979 when Dee Gruenig began providing home parties for the purchase of gifts and rubber stamps. In 1984, she established a nationally known, award winning store in Laguna Niguel, California. Other stores soon followed. A line of rubber stamps called Posh Impressions was next, and soon Dee taught scrapbooking to large sold-out classes in the first store as early as 1986.

Dee has authored or co-authored 10 books, one of them selling nearly a half million copies. She has also produced and been featured in 10 videos or DVDs and appears regularly on television. Today she designs and creates stamps, stickers, papers, tools and supplies under license for four of the most respected companies in crafts. Additionally, Dee lends her name and support to Club Posh at www.deegruenig.com , a 4,000 member group of stampers.

Visit our on-line store at **www.PoshImpressions.com**
for retail and wholesale sales.

Posh Impressions
22600-A Lambert Street, Suite 706
Lake Forest, CA, 92630
1 800 421-POSH (7674)
Fax 1 800 422 POSH
info@poshimpressions.com

Posh Impressions is the best of the best when it comes to rubberstamping. They are an icon in the industry and so talented. I am honored to have their support and respect for my books. If you're looking for an innovator in this ever-growing craft, then look no further, with Posh Impressions and the Gruenig's you have found gold. Thanks Dee and Warren for your support. May you be abundantly blessed for your kindness.   *-Linda*

■■■■■■■■■■■■■■■■■■■■■■■■■■■

RESOURCES
magazines

Simply Sentiments is a great *new* magazine whose goal is sharing innovative ideas, time saving techniques and hundreds of fresh designs with our readers. Each issue will include the following exciting sections and more... *www.simplysentiments.com*

- Fabulous Finds.
- Cookie Cutter Card
- Card Organization Solutions
- Simple Sentiments
- Ten-Minute Cards
- Design Times Two
- Crafting Cards with Children

You can subscribe online or order via phone, fax or mail in request to:

Simply Sentiments
946 Lake Road, Suite 102
Avondale, PA 19311
(610) 268-2402 (voice)
(610) 268-1518 (fax)
Electronic Mail:
Editor
editor@simplysentiments.com
Submission Inquiries
submissions@simplysentiments.com
Advertising
advertising@simplysentiments.com

Creating Keepsakes a great magazine that will showcases the latest and greatest in scrapbooking product and techniques. You'll find out all about CKU and the best in the industry.   *To subscribe to the magazine:*

Creating Keepsakes Magazine   Phone: 888/247-5282
955 Borra Place   International: 760/745-2809
Escondido, CA 92029   Fax: 760/745-7200

Be sure to add this magazine to list of must-haves! You will love all that it has to offer. Also, be sure to check out their website for much more.
www.creatingkeepsakes.com

We want to offer a big thanks to CK for allowing us to use one of their great fonts in our books. Check out their great cd's full of wonderful fonts available for sale on their website. You'll find fun, fancy and fabulous fonts to create an awesome layout your cards and scrapbooks, too.

RESOURCES
magazines

The Rubber Stamper, published eight times per year, is a rubber stampers dream come true! Every issue brings you great projects, tips and ideas. Excellent step by step projects, beautiful full color photography and tons of new product information fill each issue. Whether you are a seasoned stamper or just getting started, *you're gonna love it!*

Be sure to check out the *"Limelight Section"* for all the great new products on the market. Be sure to check out their review of my book, "The Ultimate Guide to the Perfect Word" in the January 2004 issue.

For subscription information, back issue orders, or to carry The Rubber Stamper in your store, email us at: *rssubscription@hobbypub.com*

To contact the editorial department with a question or comment about something that has appeared in The Rubber Stamper, email us at: *rseditor@hobbypub.com or call us at 1-800-260-9028*
www.rubberstamper.com

~

The Rubber Stamper
Customer Service
PO Box 102
Morganville, NJ 07751-0102 USA

RESOURCES
online stores

http://www.poshimpressions.com

http://www.ScrapCandy.com

http://www.apeekintoyesterday.com

http://www.luv2scrap.com.au/shopping.htm

http://shop.memorycreators.com/index.php

Thanks to all of the resources listed for the great support you have shown. I am so blessed to know you all.

Here's Some of Our "Perfect" Customers

BEAUTIFUL SCRAPBOOKS
BOX 12664 BENORYN
SOUTH AFRICA

CROP PAPER SCISSORS
180 COMMANCHE DR
OCEANPORT NJ

SCRAPBOOKS FROM THE HEART
502 EMBASSY OAKS #103
SAN ANTONIO TX

HEARTFELT MEMORIES
110B ASTRO SHOPPING CENTER
NEWARK DE

THE SCRAPBOOK HIDE-AWAY
1900 W. BROADWAY
MISSOULA MT

MEMORY MANIA
17424 AIRLINE HIGHWAY SUITE 7
PRAIRIEVILLE LA

THE MEMORY TRAIL
1005 PARTRIDGE PL STE 3
HELENA MT

STAMPERS WAREHOUSE
101 TOWN & COUNTRY DR #G
DANVILLE CA

MEMORY CREATORS
5511 ROGERS DRIVE
HUNTINGTON BEACH CA

MAD ABOUT SCRAPBOOKS
6253 SUNRISE BLVD
CITRUS HEIGHTS CA

MEMORIES & MORE
122 COURT ST
RICHMONDVILLE NY

SADIE'S SENTIMENTS
964 LAKE ROAD SUITE 304
AVONDALE PA

MEMORIES
1176 WEST 500 NORTH
CENTERVILLE UT

SCRAPBOOKER'S PARADISE
2001 - 10TH AVE. SW
CALGARY CA

SIMPLY SCRAPBOOKS
991 W. WILL ROGERS BLVD
CLAREMORE OK

RUNS WITH SCISSORS
331 BLUFF STREET
DUBUQUE IA

CELEBRATING MEMORIES
3158 JEFFERSON ST
NAPA CA

SMALL TOWN MEMORIES
1220 COLUMBIA BLVD SUITE #1
SAINT HELENS, OR

THE SCRAPBOOK BUG
127 FARABEE DR. N
LAFAYETTE IN

SCRAPBOOK DEPOT
606 SECOND STREET
WEBSTER CITY, IA

MEMORIES FOR THE MAKING
1325 WEST LOCKEFORD STREET
LODI CA

SCRAPPER'S DELIGHT
3333 IRVIN COBB DRIVE
PADUCAH, KY

ALL MY MEMORIES
767 E. 12300 S. SUITE B
DRAPER UT

REMEMBER WHEN SCRAPBOOKING
708 N 12TH STREET
MURRAY, KY

MEMORIES & MORE
1000 BALD HILL ROAD
WARWICK RI

2 GALS SCRAPPIN'
729 TOWER ST. S, FERGUS
ONTARIO, CANADA

Here's Some of Our "Perfect" Customers

ADVENTURES IN SCRAPBOOKING
505 SOUTH DIXIE DR.
VANDALIA, OH

ONCE UPON A MEMORY
1020 GREEN ACRES RD STE 15
EUGENE, OR

MEMORY LANE SCRAPBOOK CO.
8334 SW NIMBUS AVE
BEAVERTON, OR

A SCRAP IN TIME
151 BROCK AVE
CRESTVIEW FL

REMINISCE
411 2ND STREET
CORALVILLE IA

THANKS TO ALL OF YOU FOR YOUR
GREAT SUPPORT AND FRIENDSHIPS!

RESOURCES
designers

Scrapbook Insights specializes in web design and advertising services for scrapbook related businesses and stores. Owned and fully operated by avid scrapbookers, they know the industry and what consumers are looking for. For more information, please use the contact information below:

(419) 565-1140
www.scrapbookinsights.com
info@scrapbookinsights.com

Holly VanDyne is my website designer and I highly recommend her professionalism and artistic ability. She is a wonderful person to work with and a joy to know. If you are looking for that extra special attention to detail and someone with great vision she's the one!

Cassie English is a freelance graphic artist and custom digitizer living in Paducah, Kentucky with her husband, Joel and son Ryan. Cassie has done all types of graphic design in the past 10 years, including book design, logo design and sign design, and now embroidery design. Please feel free to contact her for more information on her design services.

Cassie English
270-898-9470
joelcassieryan@netscape.net.

177

■ ■

RESOURCES
card designers

Platinum Heart—www.platinumheart.com: Strikingly beautiful cards designed with vintage penmanship and fine art. The items are absolutely magnificent...truly a treasure you'll keep forever. Camilla Smith is an amazing artist and lady. You will love her cards and artwork. Truly unique creations, some are even on handmade paper. Absolutely charming friend!

FAVORITE QUOTES

_____

_____

_____

_____

_____

_____

_____

_____

_____

_____

_____

_____

_____

_____

If you love this book–
We know you'll be delighted
with our brand new collection of

Fabulously Fun Books

Scrappin' Expressions

Volumes 1 – 8

Designed to help transform your scrapbook pages,
stamping projects or handmade cards
into a work of art showcasing
your creative genius
February 2004

Be looking for
more books coming soon by
Linda LaTourelle
& Friends

BLUE GRASS
publishing
Mayfield, KY

Need another book?

Are you looking at your friends book right now?
Order extra copies below or go to our website at:
www.theultimateword.com
Send us an E-mail:
service@theultimateword.com

MAIL ORDER FORM

Please send _____ copy/s of:

Name: _____

Address: _____

City: _____State_____Zip: _____

E-mail: _____Phone: _____

Please include $16.95 plus $2.95 s/h (per book)
(KY add 6% tax)

Blue Grass Publishing
PO Box 634
Mayfield, KY 42066
Tel. 270.251.3600

If you're looking for a gift that will be
well-loved and used regularly order now...

The ULTIMATE Guide to the Perfect Card

Available at your local scrapbook retailer, too.